Legalized Racism

Legalized Racism

Federal Indian Policy and the End of Equal Rights for all Americans

A. R. Eguiguren

Sun on Earth Books
Heathsville, Virginia

Published by Sun on Earth Books
SOEBooks@aol.com

Library of Congress Catalog Card Number: 99-96819

Cataloging-in-Publication Data

Eguiguren, A. R.
Legalized Racism : Federal Indian Policy and the end of equal rights for all Americans / A. R. Eguiguren.
1. Indians of North America—Government relations.
2. United States—Race relations. I. Title.
E93.E38 2000
970.004'97—dc20 99-96819

ISBN 1-883378-60-5

Printed in the United States of America
Cover design by Brenda Behr

Table of Contents

Is it possible that "united" is used only
by countries that are sharply divided?

— Fintan O'Toole

Introduction

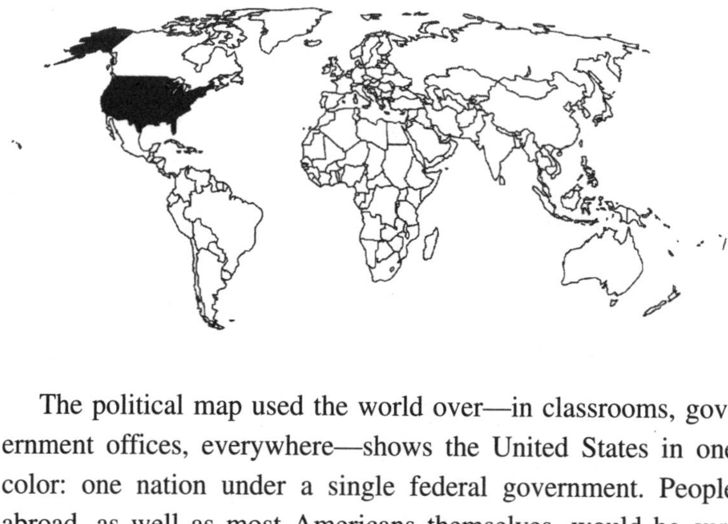

The political map used the world over—in classrooms, government offices, everywhere—shows the United States in one color: one nation under a single federal government. People abroad, as well as most Americans themselves, would be surprised to learn that there is a movement in this country intent on fragmenting the territory into various "nations."

Two hundred and ten years into the constitutional existence of our federal republic, American Indians and non-Indians are still treated as if they were citizens of different countries. Thanks to Federal Indian Policy, the United States is not one country under one law but hundreds of nations with a confusing array of laws, many of them based entirely on race.

The other nations in question are the 550-plus federally recognized Indian tribes, many of which call themselves "sovereign" and have their own constitutions. In recent years, American Indian sovereignty has become increasingly strident, demanding treatment for Native Americans that contradicts the Fourteenth Amendment to our federal Constitution, which reads, in part: "All persons born or naturalized in the United States and subject to the jurisdiction thereof, are citizens of the United States and of the State wherein they reside....No State shall...deny to any person within its jurisdiction the equal protection of the laws."

The Fourteenth Amendment was ratified on 9 July 1868. Fifty-six years later, the Citizenship Act of 1924 made all Native Americans born on U.S. soil American citizens, which they still are today. When Native Americans travel abroad, they take a U.S. passport. They represent America, not an Indian reservation. So why are they still treated differently under the law?

There are an estimated two million American Indians in the United States. A small minority of them are fanatical supporters of Indian Sovereignty—the idea that tribes are their own nations and should not have to adhere to federal laws. In many tribes, it is these sovereignty nationalists who hold the political power. They set the tone of the increasingly loud demands for tribal sovereignty and self-determination, even when most enrolled members don't want different treatment under the law.

In 1990, the Mille Lacs Ojibwe Band* of Chippewa filed a lawsuit against the State of Minnesota. It was not the first suit of its kind, but to some people it represented a taste of things to come. The suit demanded that different treatment under the law be reinstated for Band members. In essence, the plaintiffs argued that an 1837 treaty made between the Band and the United States was still active and had precedence over the Fourteenth Amendment to the U.S. Constitution.

* *Mille Lacs* is French for Thousand Lakes. *Band* is defined as a group within a given tribe, but many reports and newspaper articles use both terms interchangeably.

Introduction

This book is an introduction to the anachronistic folly that is our Federal Indian Policy. It follows the Mille Lacs lawsuit as just one example of how this policy affects all branches of government, and how it goes counter to what most Americans feel is one of the principal assets of our constitutional form of government: the idea that all citizens must be treated equally under the law.

The Mille Lacs Lawsuit

First, Wisconsin

The Mille Lacs lawsuit against Minnesota had its roots in Wisconsin, where the United States Court of Appeals for the Seventh Circuit decided, in 1983, that a number of Chippewa bands retained hunting and fishing rights in areas of the state covered by an 1837 treaty.

In 1837, a dozen Chippewa bands ceded some thirteen million acres of land (in today's Wisconsin and Minnesota) to the U.S. government. The bands ceded the land in exchange for money, goods and supplies, plus temporary hunting, fishing and gathering privileges.

This Chippewa Treaty of 1837, as it is known, covered twelve of Minnesota's contemporary counties.

Minnesota? Why Not?

Emboldened by the Wisconsin victory, which was not appealed to the U.S. Supreme Court, the Mille Lacs Band of Chippewa sued Minnesota in 1990. The 1837 treaty, they claimed, still gave them the right to hunt, fish and gather wild rice on non-reservation land in Minnesota, without regulation from the state's Department of Natural Resources (DNR).

The tribe maintained that DNR hunting and fishing rules were meant only for non-Indians (i.e., the other 98.86% of Minnesota's population).

Lake Mille Lacs, known as Minnesota's premiere sport fishing lake by virtue of being so close to the Twin Cities, is part of the 1837 ceded territory.

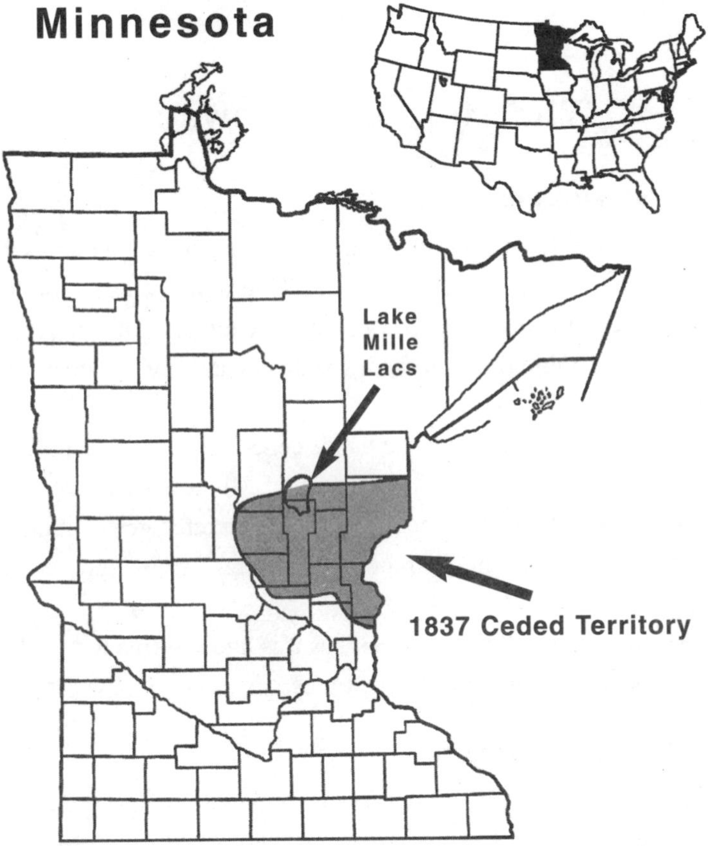

Minnesota is covered by the Eighth Circuit Court of Appeals, so the Wisconsin decision was not binding there. Hence the need for the Mille Lacs Band to sue the State of Minnesota, its Department of Natural Resources, and the Commissioner of Natural Resources. Collectively, the defendants were eventually referred to as "the State."

The trial was scheduled for 1994.

Government Relations: a Brief History

The first Indian treaty was made with the Delaware Indians in 1778. From that year until 1871, when Congress brought treaty making to an end, the United States Senate ratified 370 treaties with Indian tribes. There were at least forty-five additional treaties that were negotiated but never ratified.

After the Civil War, it became clear that expansion of United States territory by means of war with the tribes would be extremely costly. Estimates were put at one hundred thousand troops and at least a billion dollars. Treaties would be far more practical for both parties. This was decided by what was quickly becoming the more powerful side—the United States of America. Tribes had little choice but to go along with it. The alternative was a war of attrition and eventual annihilation.

The terms of the treaties varied but had some or all of the following goals in mind:

- Acquisition of land by purchase instead of by war.
- Temporary aid in the form of supplies to the tribes.
- Removal of a tribe to a reservation.
- A first step to moving Indians away from what was seen as a backward way of life and closer to the European system of civilization.

In the 1837 Treaty, the Chippewa resisted the idea of losing the land. They offered the United States a lease to the land instead, but in the negotiations leading to the 1837 Treaty, the U.S. got to make it a purchase. The band was guaranteed the privilege (not the right) to hunt, fish and gather wild rice "during the pleasure of the President."

Article V of the 1837 treaty reads: "The privilege of hunting, fishing, and gathering the wild rice, upon the lands, the rivers and the lakes included in the territory ceded, is guaranteed to the Indians, during the pleasure of the President of the United States."*

The language "during the pleasure of the President" indicates that the privilege of hunting, fishing and gathering was revocable at will.

Don Wedll, the Commissioner of Natural Resources for the Mille Lacs Band of Chippewa, didn't think so in a 1997 interview: "But what does 'pleasure of the President' mean?" he said. "I've spent sixteen years and eight million [in legal fees] trying to figure out what that means...." To the Chippewa, he added, "pleasure of the President" meant that President Van Buren was happy with the treaty.

This interpretation takes the position that the Chippewa were confused and didn't know what they were doing. But their efforts to try to get the U.S. to lease the land rather than buy it indicate otherwise.

On 14 January 1889, the United States Congress passed an "act for the relief and civilization of the Chippewa Indians in the State of Minnesota." This act became known as The Nelson Act. Its aim was very clear: "the complete cession and relinquishment in writing of all [Chippewa] title and interest in and to all the reservations of said Indians in the State of Minnesota, except the White Earth and Red Lake Reservations..."

The Mille Lacs reservation was expressly terminated by the Nelson Act. Band members were to move to the White Earth reservation, and many did. Henry Rice, the chief negotiator for the United States, explained that band members could fish and hunt off the White Earth and Red Lake Reservations, as long as they followed the same rules that other state residents were subject to.

* *For the full text of the treaty, see the Appendix.*

And this is all they are asked to do today. No one has prohibited tribal members to fish or hunt. Any citizen can get a permit.

The Nelson Act called for the allotment of land "in conformity with" the General Allotment Act of 1887 (GAA), which provided for a twenty-five year "trust period" to protect tribal members from the predatory practices of land speculators. At the end of the trust period, the individual tribal member held title to the allotment and was free to do as he wished with it.

Members of the Mille Lacs Band of Chippewa were to become allottees and, by doing so, come under the jurisdiction of the State of Minnesota under the GAA: "Upon the completion of said allotments and the patenting of the lands to said allottees," reads the Act, "each and every member of the respective bands or tribes of Indians to whom allotments have been made shall have the benefit of and be subject to the laws, both civil and criminal, of the State or Territory in which they may reside; and no Territory shall pass or enforce any law denying any such Indian within its jurisdiction the equal protection of the law…."

Both the GAA and the Nelson acts were passed not only to acquire Indian land but to protect tribes from losing *all* their land, which they would eventually have done if allotment had not been undertaken. The acts were also an effort to help the Chippewa.

The Supreme Court decision of 1913 in the case *U.S. v. Mille Lac Band of Chippewa Indians*, confirmed the disestablishment of the Mille Lacs Indian Reservation by the Nelson Act.

Some two decades later, the allotment process came to an end with the Indian Reorganization Act of 1934. John Collier, a well known champion of Indian causes, was its chief architect. In his book *From Every Zenith*, he explained his involvement when he became Commissioner of Indian Affairs, shortly after Franklin D. Roosevelt was first elected to the presidency in 1932. Collier's first action was to establish the policies he wanted to implement to, in his view, rescue Native Americans from allotment.

These policies were incorporated in a Congressional bill that became the Indian Reorganization Act (IRA) of 1934. There were hearings and consultations with the tribal leadership before the bill became law. Strangely enough, Collier, a white man, claimed that the "renaissance of the Indians as self-governing, self-respecting men came to fruition…through their thorough discussion of the Reorganization Act." However, the IRA was organized and legislated by white men. White-man Collier directed the Indians to become self-governing and self-respecting human beings. The IRA was simply one more example of the condescending attitude that the so-called Friends of the Indian has taken throughout the history of contact with indigenous peoples.

What followed the establishment of the Indian Reorganization Act was chaos. Imagine hundreds of "nations" popping up in a few years' time, many writing their own constitutions. From October of 1935 to 1940, these new constitutions—"probably the greatest in number ever written in an equivalent length of time in the history of the world," according to Collier—were drafted, voted on, and implemented.

The IRA covered all tribes except those in Alaska and Oklahoma. Many of those not covered were made eligible for benefits two years later. By 1940, 252 tribes in the country had voted on the Act: 38,000 Indians voted in favor, 24,000 against; 35,000 who were eligible to vote did not bother to do so. The Navajo voted against it. But that didn't make any difference to Collier. With his zeal, "even where the vote was against the Act, the process of self-organization went right ahead," he wrote.

Due in part to the confusion created by the IRA, which in some cases sought to enlarge Native American land holdings, the U.S. Congress established the Indian Claims Commission (ICC) in 1946 to clarify Indian claims and settle all grievances with finality. Tribes had five years (from 13 August 1946) to file claims. No claim existing before then, or not presented within that five-year period, could be submitted for consideration. Eight hundred and fifty-two claims were filed before the 1951 deadline, which was later extended into the 1970s. In thirty-two years, the ICC disbursed more than $800 million to claimants.

The Chippewa, including the Mille Lacs and Fond du Lac bands, received Indian Claims Commission payments in 1974. They totaled $9.02 million and were meant to be the final settlement for all claims arising from the 1837 Treaty. This amount was based on the value of the land for timber, which was deemed to be the use that would yield the highest price. The payment, again, was intended to settle all grievances with finality. This meant that the tribe had no further claim to the land in any shape or form.

The United States paid the $9.02 million to the tribe even though it had already paid for the land close to a hundred years earlier. According to Don Wedll, "The final payment [from the 1837 Treaty] wasn't made until 1880."

One excuse for not being satisfied with ICC rulings and awards today is that Indian lawyers were not readily available when the claims were filed, and that forced the tribes to turn to non-Indians for legal advice. This doesn't seem like a valid excuse. Today, thanks to the Native American Rights Fund (NARF), and the generous hand of the Ford Foundation, bright Native American lawyers abound. Yet, many tribes still hire non-Indian lawyers to represent them in court.

There When Needed

The Chippewa's privilege to fish and hunt in the 1837-ceded territory was revoked by presidential order in 1850. What happened between then and 1990, when the Mille Lacs Band filed its lawsuit?

The position of the Band was that the 1850 order had never been enforced, and that tribal members had gone right on netting and spearing fish—practices that are banned by the state's Department of Natural Resources today. By 1990, however, Minnesota was occasionally enforcing DNR rules, and the band used a few arrests as a pretext to sue the state.

Native sovereignty nationalists claimed that traditional fishing and hunting was tied to the Band's sovereignty. Band members deserved to be treated differently under state law because they were Indians. In other words: a non-Indian should be arrested or fined by the DNR for net-fishing but an Indian must not.

Many opponents of this double standard saw the lawsuit as the opening of exclusive, legal avenues for the eventual commercial exploitation of the Mille Lacs fishery. The nets used in commercial fishing trap and kill almost anything in their path. For this reason, the Bush administration banned imports of fish caught with nets in July of 1992. And almost a decade earlier, several Minnesota residents had fought hard for the passage of the Omnibus Fishing Bill of 1983. The bill ended commercial fishing of game fish in the state, except on the Red Lake Indian Reservation (in northwestern Minnesota), where the tribe was allowed to continue to exploit its commercial fishery, and where the tribe, not the state's DNR, regulates the fishery. There, the catch fell from 800,000 pounds of fish to 60,000 in just a few years. Three hundred full-time netters depleted the stock to a point where tribal fisheries officials became alarmed and a Council member warned of "ruin" and "collapse."

As a result, Red Lake could not support a sport fishery or resort industry like Lake Mille Lacs. The largest industry in Mille Lacs County (approximately $100 million per year) is tourism, most of it thanks to the resorts on Lake Mille Lacs, which is the only lake in the county with substantial tourism infrastructure.

In the early 1980s, sportsmen and resort owners formed the Mille Lacs Lake Advisory Association (MLLAA) to push for new conservation measures and safeguard the future of the sport fishery. Almost a decade later, when the Band filed its lawsuit, MLLAA members were accused of being racist for their insistence that state rules apply to all citizens—Indian and non-Indian—using the lake.

With the 1990 lawsuit, Band members indicated that only they should be allowed to gill-net fish, having an open option to fish commercially at any point in the future. Their claim was that they might need the revenue to survive.

But there was more to it. "If we have the right to commercially fish, we want our rights," said Jim Pence, the Mille Lacs Band's solicitor general, in a 1992 interview. "Whether or not commercial fishing is economically viable is a different question," he added.

Commercially caught walleye fish is worth almost nothing to the local economy. Nets catch the fish, and the harvest gets dumped in trucks and driven out of town for very little money. In contrast, sport fishing supports local communities by bringing tourists to the lake. These tourists pay for hotel accommodations, meals, fishing licenses, and other necessities from local stores. They make the economy work.

Today, there is more than one economic engine in Mille Lacs County. Tourism from the sport fishing industry is the most significant. The other one is the Mille Lacs Casino, which is owned by the Band. Marge Anderson, the Mille Lacs Chippewa's chief executive, told *Forbes* magazine in November of 1998: "My parents taught me to never, *ever* take a handout, especially from the federal government," presumably because she wanted to take credit for the Band's economy. Gross revenue from the Band's two northern Minnesota casinos topped $200 million in 1998. The Mille Lacs invested ten million dollars to acquire forty percent of the stock of the Indian Wells bottled-water company. In 1996, the Band had issued over $80 million worth of redevelopment bonds to build infrastructure and expand a casino.

Yet, three bureaucratic juggernauts—the Departments of Interior, Housing, and Health—drop millions of dollars of American citizens' tax money to the 3,000-member Band every year. The Department of Housing and Urban Development alone gave the Band $4.5 million in 1995 to build forty houses on the Mille Lacs "Reservation." That works out to about $110,000 per house. Who were the lucky recipients?

Whether the Mille Lacs 1837 Treaty lawsuit came about as a resource or economic issue, a dialog on the topic was never viable because of the issue of race. To the Band's supporters, everyone who was not on their side was a racist, and that attitude ended all possibilities for a friendly solution.

The State of Things

The Non-Indian View

For most Americans, and indeed, the world, the popular view of who American Indians are has been—for the current and recent generations, at least—molded completely by stories of cowboys and Indians, whether in print, comics, or the movies. Alcoholism, powwows, drumming, mysticism, sacred dancing, vibrant whelping, victimhood, feathers, regalia, and casinos are just a few of the stereotypes applied to the 550-plus federally recognized tribes in the country.

The collective perception is that American Indians were dispossessed of their land, decimated by war and disease, and taken advantage of.

In the 1960s, European journalists were said to be fascinated with the demonstrations made by Native Americans to end colonialism in the U.S. The goal of the demonstrations was freedom for American Indian nations. According to Native American scholar Vine Deloria, Jr., "The trauma of the French in Indo-China and Algeria had made a deep impression on the people of Europe." So they understood the point of view of the American Indian, Deloria said, while non-Indian Americans didn't have a clue.

But European imperialism was hardly relevant and quite a different thing: Not all of England lived in Ghana or Nigeria; or all of France in Algeria.

There is no doubt that Americans possess a great deal of sympathy for Native Americans. In any informal poll, no matter how ignorant respondents are of the subject, they almost always show sympathy toward the American Indian. Questions such as, "Should Indians have the *same* fishing rights as whites?" "Have Native Americans been an oppressed people?" "Should the federal government help them in any possible way?" will all be answered with a solid "Yes."

If the pollster is feeling manipulative, he can pepper the poll with questions such as, "Should Native Americans be helped economically by the federal government to make up for the suffering inflicted on them by the white man?" Most respondents, regardless of race, will still answer "Yes." Asked, "For how long?" Answer: "Until conditions are equal." The goal is equality, or so people think.

Some non-Indians go as far as calling the federal government "evil" for doing whatever has been done to Native Americans. But the federal government is not an entity with a life all its own. Citizens are supposed to run it through their congressional representatives, senators and tax contributions. The so-called "Federal responsibility to Indians" means nothing other than the whole country's responsibility to the tribes. But no one alive today is responsible for what somebody's ancestors did to someone else's ancestors many decades ago. We are only responsible for what is happening today, and that means that the federal government has responsibilities to all American citizens, not just American Indians.

Equal treatment under the law, as stipulated in the Fourteenth Amendment to the U.S. Constitution, is not the goal of Native sovereignty nationalists. During the Civil Rights movement, many freedom fighters were baffled to learn that the Native American leadership involved in the fight for civil rights was not interested in equal treatment under the law for all Americans. Their goal was not a Civil Rights Act but sovereignty for Indian nations and eventual severance from United States territory.

The Nixon Administration facilitated many of the acts of civil disobedience and illegal actions perpetrated by Native sovereignty nationalists in the 1970s. Soon after taking office, President Nixon wrote in a special introduction to the *North Dakota Law Review*:

"...White House efforts have helped to produce Congressional action beneficial to the Indians—restoration of the Blue Lake lands, authorization of the Navajo Community College, appropriations to promote Indian health, demonstration aid to urban Indian centers, and the Alaska Native Claims Settlement. But much more remains to be done."

Howard Hanson, a Minneapolis businessman who began to organize opposition to commercial fishing by white netters in Minnesota lakes in 1980, has developed a theory on why President Nixon was so eager to do "much more" for Native Americans. When the Omnibus Fishing Bill of 1983 passed, Hanson maintains, the bill ended commercial fishing in the state and with it the supply line for hundreds of seafood restaurants owned by multi-national corporations. The corporations had anticipated the bill for over a decade, and had developed a plan: the funding of Native sovereignty nationalists through non-profit foundations. The money would be used by the sovereignty nationalists to file lawsuits against various states demanding restoration of treaty "rights." Once the tribes won their cases in court—and there was every indication that they would, due to increasing judicial activism—American Indians would have access to up to fifty percent of the targeted fish without state regulation. The corporations would then buy the fish from the tribes to supply their growing chains of restaurants. The Omnibus

Fishing Bill, being nothing more than state legislation, would have no power over the Bureau of Indian Affairs and the Department of Interior.

The plan, according to Hanson, was easily implemented during the Nixon Administration because Nixon owed his election to campaign money supplied by the largest shareholders of the same multi-national corporations.

Hanson has spent twenty years studying and documenting political-action committees, soft-money contributions, corruption at the Bureau of Indian Affairs, and certain foundation grants that he considers to have a political agenda that perpetuates Federal Indian Policy and undermines the equal treatment of all citizens under the law. He has called for a thorough investigation of campaign finance to uncover the real motives behind large personal contributions, but no public official or enterprising reporter has offered to challenge the system yet.

Twenty Points

During the Nixon Administration, a group of Native sovereignty nationalists produced what eventually became known as the Twenty Points—a shopping list of Indian demands.

Since the Nixon Administration had a good record with such demands—it had restored tribal lands, among other things—the American Indian Movement (AIM) expected the Twenty Points to have a good reception. Summarized, the very repetitive Twenty Points were:

1. Restoration of constitutional treaty-making authority with tribes.
2. Establishment of a Commission to make new treaties.
3. A nationally televised event with Congress and the

President to tell the American people about federal recognition of tribes as independent political and national entities.

4. The creation of a commission to review treaty commitments and violations.
5. Resubmission to the Senate of the many unratified treaties for ratification.
6. Governance of Native Americans exclusively by treaty relations with the United States.
7. Mandatory relief (via injunctions) against treaty violations by non-Indians.
8. Judicial recognition of Indians' rights to interpret treaties, and a law requiring the U.S. Supreme Court to hear all treaty violation cases.
9. Reconstruction of congressional committees dealing with Indian affairs so that only one committee acts as liaison with all tribes.
10. Restoration of a 110-million-acre Native land base via land reform.
11. Restoration of rights to Indians terminated by enrollment.
12. Do away with all state control over Indian land by repealing laws enacted under Public Law 280 [state jurisdiction over tribes].
13. Make any crime committed by non-Indians against Indians a federal offense tried by a federal Indian grand jury.
14. Abolition of the Bureau of Indian Affairs.
15. Replacement of the Bureau of Indian Affairs with an "Office of Federal Indian Relations and Community Reconstruction."
16. Set Indian "priorities and purpose" for the new Office of Federal Indian Relations and Community Reconstruction.
17. Removal of all tribes from state taxation.

18. Legal protection for "Indian religious expression."
19. Consolidation of Indian leadership at local levels.
20. Increased federal funding for Indian health, housing, education, employment and economic development programs.

Some of the points were so extreme that the demands went nowhere. Native sovereignty nationalists hardly ever mention the Twenty Points anymore, though they still stand by what they represent.

Who's Boss?

Tribal members are American citizens and under the jurisdiction of United States laws—except for Federal Indian Policy. First established to deal with "the Indian problem," Federal Indian Policy has always been an enemy of equal treatment under the law for Indians and non-Indians.

Under the policy, the federal government, not the states in which Native Americans reside, is in charge of government relations with the tribes. This has placed the states at odds with the federal government on issues like conservation, land management, and natural resources.

When in the early 1970s the United States government decided to restore tribal sovereignty, it brought a suit on behalf of the Leech Lake Band of Chippewa against the State of Minnesota. The goal was to have the usufructuary rights given to the Chippewa in an 1855 Treaty restored to the Band. Usufructuary rights are those that are of "limited duration on the property of another."

So far, the federal government has joined more than six lawsuits in Minnesota and Wisconsin on behalf of several Chippewa bands. The goal of these suits has been to override the regulatory powers of both states in regard to fishing, hunting and gathering on public land. The United States government (in reality, the Department of Justice as directed by the President) claims that it is only enforcing treaties made under the so-called Treaty Clause of the Constitution. But many believe that the treaties signed with tribes have been abrogated or rendered irrelevant by acts of Congress and other political processes.

In the case of the 1837 Treaty, there were at least four of these processes by which the treaty's hunting and fishing privileges were extinguished:

- A 6 February 1850 Executive Order signed by President Zachary Taylor. (Executive Branch.)
- A treaty signed in 1855. (Executive and Legislative Branches.)
- The Nelson Act of 1889. (Legislative Branch.)
- Payments made to the tribe by the Indian Claims Commission. (Legislative Branch.)

If a political process created the 1837 Treaty, a judicial one was to decide what effect, if any, the four points above had had on it. By some strange twist in law, the U.S. government was on the side of treating citizens differently according to race, and of pushing the idea of Native American sovereignty.

Don Wedll, the Commissioner of Natural Resources for the Mille Lacs Band of Chippewa, has said that there are three sovereign entities in the United States. "One is the United States government, which has supreme power, another is state governments and a third is tribal governments."

Puerto Rico: A Model?

In practice, there are more than three so-called sovereign entities in the United States. A number of them have fallen into permanent limbo under the "U.S. Territories and Possessions" status. The U.S. administers them through all sorts of conflicting rules.

During a December, 1998, vote for defining the status of Puerto Rico, Anibal Acevedo Vila, the head of the island's Popular Democratic Party, said, "We are not Americans....We are U.S. citizens and we're proud of that. But we are Puerto Ricans, and if we become a state we will lose our identity, our culture, our language."

The island of Puerto Rico was ceded to the U.S. by Spain in 1898. Its current political status of Commonwealth was organized in 1952. Puerto Ricans are indeed U.S. citizens (since 1917), but they pay no federal taxes. They can vote for President and members of Congress if they live in one of the fifty U.S. states, but not if they live on the island. They are subject to military service. They have no sovereignty other than in symbols—an Olympic team and their own Miss Universe contestant.

Nine billion dollars of federal aid expenditures go every year to the 3.8 million people who live on the island. Yet, sixty percent of them live below the poverty line. Nine billion dollars is more than the U.S. Agency for International Development (USAID) budgets annually for programs in all foreign countries combined.

Puerto Ricans' U.S. citizenship hangs by a thread. Unless they agree by plebiscite to join the Union as the fifty-first state, the U.S. Congress can decide at any moment that Puerto Ricans are no longer citizens of the United States. Their citizenship, according to former U.S. Attorney General Dick Thornburgh, is "granted by statute and not fully protected by the U.S. Constitution." This shows how fragile the political status of those who live on the island is. They are fully at the whim of Congress, just as the American colonies were at the whim of Great Britain before the Revolutionary War, or Native Americans are today of the Department of Interior.

The simplest solution to this situation is to do away with territorial status and make those affected by it real citizens of the United States, with equal treatment under the law. A barrier to this solution, however, is the money involved in maintaining the status quo. Who would want to change things as they are with all that federal aid coming in every year?

That is why Puerto Ricans voted "None of the above" in December of 1998, while still claiming to oppose their current status. It was a way to protest against the island's relationship with the United States while maintaining the privileges, money, and rights.

Puerto Rico is not alone. There is Guam, American Samoa, the Virgin Islands, and other lesser known territories. Originally, territorial status was created as a temporary first step on the way to statehood. Newly acquired land became a territory while preparing to follow the provisions in the Northwest Ordinance of 1787, which established the steps for achieving equal status with the rest of the states.

The U.S. Constitution also hints at the transient character of territorial status: "The Congress shall have Power to dispose of and make all needful Rules and Regulations respecting the Territory or other Property belonging to the United States." (Article IV, Sec. 3, Cl. 2.) Thanks to this so-called Property Clause, the U.S. Congress has plenary power over territories and the people who live on them, and that is why it can decide tomorrow that Puerto Ricans are no longer U.S. citizens, and why the Founding Fathers intended such potentially despotic power to be only temporarily held by Congress. It was too close to the power once held over the American colonies by Great Britain, and the idea behind the U.S. Constitution was to give the power to the people, not the Congress.

Israel

Native sovereignty nationalists use Israel as an example of their rights to a homeland. "No longer content to leave their fate in the hands of other people," writes Native American scholar Vine Deloria, Jr., in *Behind the Trail of Broken Treaties*, "the Jews in Israel began an insurrection against the British administration to achieve political control of their own lives." This refers to the United Nations resolution that created separate states for Jews and Arabs in 1947.

"If the U.S. can recognize the historic claim of a specific people to land in the Middle East," adds Deloria, "there is no reason in fact or logic for it to continue to ignore the claim of the native Americans to territorial sovereignty over a small portion of their historical land."

The comparison seems forced when historical timing is taken into consideration. Israel finally became Israel (after almost a century of active Zionism) in good part because of the immediacy created by the atrocities committed against Jews during World War II. No similar, desperate fear of pogroms had existed for Native Americans in more than seventy years when Deloria made the comparison. Neither are Native Americans persecuted today.

Deloria continues: "The world watched with almost evil fascination as Adolf Hitler assumed power in Germany and began an extensive campaign to deny German Jews their legal and civil rights." The idea here is to compare Germany's treatment of Jews during World War II with the United States' treatment of its native peoples in the second half of the twentieth century. Deloria offers no evidence to justify his choice of words. Certainly, America was not watching with "evil fascination."

Whatever one thinks of Israel, why would any group in the United States want to emulate it? The conflict between Palestinians and Israelis since Israel's founding is not the type of social development the U.S. should strive for. Israel has unfortunately not been an example of a land living in peace.

Yet "Nation" status, as recognized by the United Nations, is what Native sovereignty nationalists want. The reason: once considered voting members of the United Nations, the new, racially-created countries would be able to file accusations of genocide against the United States under the rules of the UN's Genocide Convention. "Federal policy for the major portion of this century has been oriented toward the systematic destruction of Indian communities," writes Deloria, qualifying Federal Indian Policy as genocide.

Citizenship

Are American Indians citizens of the United States, or are they dual citizens of 500-plus nations within the U.S? Senator Ben Nighthorse Campbell of Colorado, who chairs the Senate Committee on Indian Affairs and is a member of the Northern Cheyenne Tribe, has said, "My own view is that they can be both, should be both, and are both."

The State Department maintains that Native American citizenship is not legally recognized either in the U.S. or other countries. But the Bureau of Indian Affairs says that "Indians…are members of their respective Tribes and thus have dual citizenship."

Vine Deloria, Jr., takes another position in *Behind the Trail of Broken Treaties*. His thesis is that Indian tribes "remain in a very real sense foreign nations with respect to the United States." This is shown, he says, by the fact that treaties were signed between the two parties, and treaties are only signed between sovereign nations. So it follows that American Indians must gain their independence. Except, is that what they really want—to no longer be Americans? Or is that what Native sovereignty nationalists want?

The call for dual citizenship could be said to have started during Termination. Termination was an earnest effort to end the perception of Territorial status for U.S. reservations. The policy, established in 1944 but best defined in 1953 with Public Law 280, aimed to end federal services and programs to all Indian reservations. Public Law 280 was meant to allow the states to take over the jurisdiction of the tribes and get the federal government out of the "Indian business" once and for all. "Termination" was an unfortunate term. Integration would have been a better one.

The National Congress of American Indians (NCAI) was set against termination. It asked for a dual identity for American Indians that included both American citizenship and tribal membership. NCAI was instrumental in the organization of Indian interests groups in the 1960s. The groups' demands included the mutually exclusive goals of treaty rights and American citizenship, the latter of which all members already had.

NCAI

The National Congress of American Indians (NCAI) is "the oldest and largest national (Indian) organization, established in 1944 and comprised of representatives of and advocates for national, regional, and local Tribal concerns....NCAI is dedicated to the preservation and protection of treaty rights of tribes nationally."

—Midwest Treaty Network

Attempts at Settlement

Out-of-Court Gymnastics

If the old treaties were signed out of convenience and expediency for the goals of the U.S. government, modern-day treaties (often called "out-of-court settlements") follow the same pattern. The difference is that only a handful of people are well served by these modern settlements, especially when they are negotiated in secret.

After the Mille Lacs Band of Ojibwe filed its lawsuit in 1990, the Minnesota Department of Natural Resources decided to negotiate a settlement, perhaps because it was less work than researching the facts which made plain the reality that the tribe's suit had cracks in it.

When the settlement agreement was finally brought into the open as it went before the Minnesota State Legislature for ratification, supporters maintained that it allowed a fair conclusion to the problem without having to go to trial. Litigation would cost too much money, they claimed, and violence could break out in the state, as it had in Wisconsin during the trial in the Wisconsin treaty case.

Arne Carlson, Minnesota's Governor at the time, urged the state legislature to approve the agreement, while a few active citizens did their best to bring the thirty-page proposed settlement to the public's attention because no information about it had been given to the public until after the negotiations had concluded.

Few Minnesotans knew at the time that the settlement would…

- pay the Band $8.6 to $10 million in cash.
- transfer up to 15,000 acres of unspecified Minnesota public land to the band. This land, including mineral rights, would be placed in trust status, off the public tax roles.
- expand the 3,800 acres of Mille Lacs trust land into the 61,000-acre Mille Lacs Reservation that had existed before 1889.
- allow band members to fish, hunt and gather without state regulation, and take up to fifty percent of the harvestable resources in most of the treaty area.
- establish an exclusive tribal fishing zone (essentially, an Apartheid system) on Lake Mille Lacs.
- place entire townships and thousands of property owners inside reservation boundaries, subject to tribal jurisdiction under a government system in which they would have no right to vote because of their race.
- allow the Mille Lacs Band to net and spear fish in six other lakes of the territory involved in the lawsuit, and also in sections of the St. Croix and Rum rivers.

The few active citizens who made an effort to inform the public were quickly labeled "misguided" and "racist." In their defense, Howard Hanson, the Minneapolis businessman, said, "This is America and it's legal to try to effect change. That's what we're doing. We want to get all the facts to the public, and effect change."

They had good reason to do so. Allowing the tribe to fish without DNR oversight meant that band members could use gill nets when fishing. The DNR and the Great Lakes Indian Fish and Wildlife Commission had both noted that gill nets with even a 1.75-inch mesh would catch the large breeding-stock fish that supported the Mille Lacs fishery.

If anything, the proposed settlement showed what was really behind the 1990 lawsuit—an effort to grab as much land and access to public natural resources as the state legislature would bear. Treaty rights were just the confounding legal excuse, the ruse. As state Senator Daniel L. Stevens (District 17, Mora) commented later, "Not one member of the Mille Lacs Band has ever been denied a Minnesota fishing license to fish according to the regulations established by the Minnesota DNR." Band members already had the right to fish, just as any other citizen of the state.

Hidden Agenda

Several legal documents submitted in the case kept on referring to "the Mille Lacs Indian Reservation." This was probably the most important hidden agenda of the settlement for the Band—the act of reestablishing the boundaries of a 61,000-acre reservation that had been first defined in the Treaty of 1855 and later disestablished by the Nelson Act. The Band's 1990 lawsuit had not even addressed the reservation issue. The reference had been added now to the settlement's wish list.

In a 1995 letter to the Lake Mille Lacs Association, Inc., Governor Arne Carlson wrote, "You…asked about my position on the boundaries of the Mille Lacs Reservation. Minnesota's position has been, and is today, that the Mille Lacs Reservation was disestablished through later federal treaties and laws."

Later still, in 1998, and by unanimous opinion, the U.S. Supreme Court ruled for Alaska in *State of Alaska v. Native Village of Venetie*, stating that a paramount consideration in whether an Indian reservation has been disestablished is the Congress' intent in laws passed, as was the case with the Nelson Act for the Mille Lacs Reservation.

The Department of Interior, through its Bureau of Indian Affairs, still disagrees. In a 1998 letter to a concerned Minnesotan, a BIA employee wrote: "…you ask whether the 'old' reservation of the Mille Lacs Band still exists. Our review indicates that the Mille Lacs Indian Reservation continues to exist today as it was described in the Treaty of 1855. *There is no indication that the reservation boundaries have ever been diminished since then….*" [Emphasis added.]

Even religious groups jumped on the bandwagon of ignoring the Fourteenth Amendment. The Evangelical Lutheran Church of America called for "advocacy in the area of Native American treaty rights, tribal sovereignty, and religious freedom….including advocacy for justice for Native Americans." An extreme contradiction in terms since, as historian Balint Vazsonyi notes, "A person's rights are best secured by conceding the very same rights to every other person under the same jurisdiction." And Treaty rights do no such thing when they only apply to less than one percent of the U.S. population.

"The Mille Lacs Band of Ojibwe," the Church's statement continued, "and the State of Minnesota (through the efforts of the Department of Natural Resources) have negotiated an agreement regarding rights guaranteed in the Treaty of 1837. This Agreement avoids costly litigation regarding the Treaty. The Band has spent more than ten years in research and legal preparation to pursue its rights through the courts. It is acting in the context of the precedent established in Wisconsin regarding the same 1837 Treaty. In that case, the courts ruled in favor of the Ojibwe people."

The Church referred to the settlement as honorable and just, conforming to the economic and social realities of today. But that was not the point. A settlement out of court would only invite future lawsuits, just like the decision of Wisconsin not to appeal the case had invited legal action by the Band against Minnesota.

"It seems to us that the underlying issue is not a question of walleyes and nets: *it is a matter of justice,...*" the letter went on. "Consequently, we will advocate for the ratification of this Agreement at the Minnesota State Legislature."

The Band's lawsuit had been billed as a crisis, one that must be resolved quickly by secret negotiations because telling too many people would just delay a decision and cost too much money.

In the end, the public would not be fooled. Once word got out of what a settlement would mean for private property owners, public opposition to treaty rights grew. A sporting association named The Hunting and Angling Club was instrumental in urging the Legislature to reject the fishing-rights settlement between the Band and the state's Department of Natural Resources. Minnesotans had realized that this was not a local issue. If the agreement passed the Legislature, other lawsuits would soon be filed in connection to treaties relevant to other parts of the state.

State governments have a legal obligation to manage public land and natural resources for the benefit of all state residents. With the settlement, the State of Minnesota was prepared to give away most of its power to enforce natural-resource management in the Mille Lacs 1837 Treaty area. It was ready to transfer jurisdiction of a significant amount of land from the legitimate government of the citizens of Minnesota to that of a small ethnic group.

Media reports lacked the kind of objective analysis that the Mille Lacs case required. Joe Fellegy, a local historian and columnist, said, "If any other entity had jurisdictional designs on large parts of Minnesota, I would bet that entity would be caught up in the usual and typical and legitimate press scrutiny of the issues involved. The leaders would be questioned, and they would be held accountable for their agenda, and how that agenda would affect people in the area. I don't think we've seen that here. In fact, I can't recall a newspaper challenging a single statement a band official has made."

Bud Grant, the well known former Minnesota Vikings coach, got involved in support of equal treatment under the law for all citizens. His participation gave the issue a much broader public exposure.

Citizens React

On 15 April 1992, The Hunting and Angling Club held a rally on the steps of the Minnesota State Capitol, in St. Paul. It was the most effective way to publicly demand information about the settlement from state officials.

Rally participants asked Governor Arne Carlson and Attorney General Hubert H. Humphrey, III, to make sure that the State of Minnesota…

- distribute a fact sheet outlining what was at stake in the Treaty case;
- no longer engage in secret negotiations giving away public land and resources;
- devote adequate attention and resources to prepare for the case;
- file in support of the rights of the landowners, counties, and sports clubs to join, intervene or participate in the lawsuit; and

- have the benefit of a Governor and Attorney General thoroughly familiar with the strengths and weaknesses of the State's legal position and the long-term effects of a negotiated settlement.

The Hunting and Angling Club committed itself to support the legal defense of the landowners who were intervened (i.e., allowed to join) in the case. Steve Froehle, an attorney with the Minneapolis law firm Persian, MacGregor and Thompson, submitted the intervention documents.

Froehle also discussed with William A. Szotkowski, the Special Assistant to Minnesota's Attorney General, the idea of having the State represent the interests of landowners in the case. But Szotkowski replied that, "As we discussed, the State is authorized to represent the collective interests of its citizens in this matter....Private property owners clearly have individual interests that extend beyond the State's interests in providing access to and managing the public's resources....The State cannot represent the interest of private landowners."

This made little sense. When hundreds of state citizens are affected by property rights issues brought on by the federal government, who is there to turn to if not the state government?

Land and business owners in the Mille Lacs 1837 Treaty area depend on the hunting and fishing industry for their economic survival. The main thrust of intervention was that a few citizens should not be made to bear the burden of treaty rights claims. Everyone is for "helping the Indian" in some nebulous sort of way. But what property owner in the country would still be so willing to help if the help involved the use or taking of *his* land and resources? It is too easy to make redress with other people's property.

Of course, the property rights of Native Americans, when the tribes were first dispossessed of their land, were not respected, either. But that is not the current landowners' fault. The mess of treaty rights wasn't created by them. Nor can the tribes of today be blamed for them. So-called treaty rights are the result of gross mismanagement of government affairs, past and present.

The end result of treaty litigation in Wisconsin was the best reason for opposing a settlement in Minnesota. As a result of the arrangement with the Chippewa, the citizens of Wisconsin had...

- seen the reduction of walleye limits in some of the affected lakes;
- suffered the closing of resorts and businesses in the ceded territory because of the inevitable downturn in tourism (no tourist wants to be subject to government-sanctioned racial discrimination);
- seen their tourism industry sustain losses of over $10 million and more than 300 jobs per year;
- watched property values plummet nearly $25 million in the ceded territory.

As Bud Grant said, the agreement in Wisconsin had "turned out to be a disaster for much of the northern part of the state," all because Wisconsin had not had the determination to appeal the case to the U.S. Supreme Court.

The citizens of Minnesota were not about to make the same mistake.

Fear Tactics

Jim Pence, Solicitor General for the Mille Lacs Band of Chippewa, tried to scare Minnesotans into accepting the settlement to avoid potentially heavier losses in court. In a 1992 interview, he said: "Historically, courts have said in these types of cases that Indians are entitled to half the harvestable resource....There have been sixteen major treaty rights cases in recent years and the Indians have won them all."

Statistical data compiled by Robert N. Clinton and published in the *Connecticut Law Review* presented a completely different picture:

- Between 1986 and 1990, tribal interests had prevailed in the U.S. Supreme Court twenty percent of the time;
- since 1990, in only fourteen percent of the cases.

Jim Pence was probably referring to cases at the district court level. And the district court in the Mille Lacs case was believed to be strongly biased. It would not even allow the landowners to intervene in the case. (A reversal by the Eighth Circuit Court of Appeals was required to give the landowners their intervention rights.)

While everyone waited for a solution to the impasse, a number of supporters of the settlement option resorted to lowest-denominator media attacks. One critic even saw it fit to comment on Hall-of-Famer Bud Grant's coaching abilities, saying that Grant had a poor record—inferring that the record showed how Grant just didn't have what it took to deal with treaty-rights issues.

What Was Really at Stake

One must look at Wisconsin again, where the Chippewa were legally allowed to hunt and fish on public land on the ceded territory. Band members there, less than one percent of the state's population, could…

- take up to fifty percent of the "harvestable surplus" of fish and game;
- gill-net and spear fish—a practice forbidden to all other citizens of Wisconsin.

Predictions for what would happen in the Mille Lacs ceded territory if the settlement passed the legislature were even more ominous. Tourism in Mille Lacs was big. It supported some 1,700 employees. Sport fishing and hunting brought in $34,620,000 a year.

An economist for the landowners estimated that if the Band was allowed to take up to fifty percent of the ceded territory's natural resources, the local economy would lose $17,300,000 in tourism revenue, 863 full-time jobs, and $41,200,000 in property values.

Joe Karpen, one of the affected landowners who had bought his resort in 1979, said, "The resort industry is the biggest industry in [Mille Lacs] county. Very few businesses would survive without the lake."

The most insidious aspect of the 1990 lawsuit and the ensuing settlement negotiations, however, was the animosity it generated between Indians and non-Indians. Wasn't that reason enough to stop the government-backed process of random reparations not only in Minnesota but in the country as a whole? Even Ojibwe members had testified against the settlement. It was destroying the Mille Lacs community.

Since racial issues are such a delicate matter, calls began for the federal government to start reviewing Federal Indian Policy at once, and for the courts to resolve all disagreements with finality. But that was an old song. The Indian Claims Commission had been established to do just that, and here they were—the states of the Union—more than fifty years later, still being sued by tribes that still wanted past wrongs to be turned into more rights.

"Many of these wrongs have been corrected over the years," Bud Grant said, "and compensation paid. But it always keeps coming back."

Native sovereignty nationalists didn't see it that way. Settling treaty provisions did *not* end the constitutional rights of the tribes, they said. Those constitutional rights had been established by treaty and could not be taken away. Treaties, they said, limit the power of the United States over Indian Americans because, constitutionally, treaties are the Supreme Law of the Land.

Back to Court

The reality of legal costs today forces a great many litigants to settle out of court. But what happens when one side strongly believes that the case has no merit, that settling it out of court is the same as recognizing that there is merit in it?

Out-of-court settlement is the goal of most nuisance lawsuits: The plaintiffs are not really interested in justice but in getting away with some sort of compensation. The problem with agreeing to such compensation is that it invites more lawsuits.

So the state of Minnesota, thanks to the clear opposition of its citizens, said "No" to the settlement, and the parties were on their way to federal court. By April, nine of the twelve Minnesota counties affected and six Minnesota landowners had joined the State as defendants in the case.

An organization called PERM (Proper Economic Resource Management) would eventually raise more than one million dollars to cover the landowners' legal fees. Mark Rotz, PERM's president, led their "Save Minnesota" campaign.

The DOJ Joins The Fray

Federal statute 25 U.S.C. § 175 requires that the United States Attorney represent American Indians in "all suits at law and in equity." But there was more than the statute to the Department of Justice's involvement. The more obvious reason was that current government policy called for supporting tribal governments because of the "long-standing moral obligation of the United States government to guard the rights...of our country's tribal peoples as zealously as we protect the rights of all Americans," as Vice President Albert Gore wrote in a letter to Howard Hanson. "Please be assured that the President and I will be working as hard as possible to fulfill that obligation," he added.

Executive Branch moral crusades such as this one are usually orchestrated through a little-known public servant with the title of Solicitor General (SG). The SG works at the Department of Justice but also has a permanent chamber in the Supreme Court. His role is to almost exclusively represent the Executive Branch in the Supreme Court.

In *The Tenth Justice*, a book about the post of Solicitor General, Lincoln Caplan describes the SG as operating in "a sphere of government that is invisible to almost all citizens," and whose influence is undeniable. "During the 1983 Term of the Supreme Court," he writes, "of the 3,878 petitions for writs of certiorari (the form in which most parties ask the Court to review a case) submitted by lawyers across the country, the Justices granted only 3 percent. Of petitions from the Solicitor General, they approved 79 percent." The 1998/1999 Term saw those rates go down to 1 percent and 40 percent, respectively.

Another reason the Department of Justice might want to get involved was the question of jurisdiction. Under the Eleventh Amendment to the U.S. Constitution, the State of Minnesota might ask the Band's lawsuit to be dismissed.

The Eleventh Amendment is brief: "The Judicial power of the United States shall not be construed to extend to any suit in law or equity, commenced or prosecuted against one of the United States by Citizens of another State, or by Citizens or Subjects of any Foreign State."

It is difficult to understand why the federal government would fight the citizens of Minnesota in court with the goal of establishing different treatment under the law for a racially defined group of people. It is not what most Americans have been brought up to believe in regard to the virtues of American democratic principles and common sense.

The federal government had purchased the Mille Lacs ceded territory for $875,000 in 1837. The Chippewa had collected additional payments for so-called harvest rights in 1855, 1863, 1864, and 1888. And now the government was giving the Band, through the Department of Interior's Bureau of Indian Affairs, funds to sue Minnesota over those same harvest rights? And the DOJ was *joining* the Band in the lawsuit?

In December of 1993, Federal District Judge Diana Murphy upheld orders to allow the U.S. Justice Department to intervene as a plaintiff in the 1837 Treaty lawsuit. She also denied the Save Lake Mille Lacs Association, which represented more than 125 sports' and landowners' groups, to intervene in the case as a defendant. With Judge Murphy presiding the case at the Federal District level, it was obvious what her decision would be just a few months later.

Going Through Phases

The district court decided to split the Mille Lacs case into two phases.

- Phase I would concern itself with whether the Mille Lacs Band indeed had the privilege to hunt, fish, and gather in the 1837 ceded territory free of state regulation.
- Phase II would take place only if Phase I was ruled in favor of the Band. This second Phase would establish what percentage of Minnesota's natural resources in the ceded territory would go to the tribe.

Then came what lawyers call the discovery part of the case. During this process, all parties to the lawsuit are allowed to serve each other with requests (in writing) for information pertinent to the case. Questions must be answered within a set period of time.

Depositions are taken during discovery. Jeff Chaffee, the attorney representing the coalition of county defendants, estimated that there would be some twelve expert witnesses giving depositions. Lay witnesses were also being considered.

Jim Genia, the Band's Solicitor General, filed motions asking the court to dismiss most of the State's arguments for defense before the case was even heard. Judge Diana Murphy complied, issuing a summary judgement in the spring of 1994 (later reversed by the Eighth Circuit Court of Appeals).

Diana Rules

The case was finally heard in Federal Court from 13 June until 6 July 1994. The arguments concentrated on the 1837 Treaty privileges and how they had been affected by the 1850 Presidential Order and the treaty of 1855.

Because it seemed obvious which way the ruling would go, the defendants (the State of Minnesota, nine counties, and six landowners) requested the right to immediately appeal the ruling if it turned out to be favorable to the Band.

Denied. Judge Murphy ruled that no appeals would be taken until after completion of Phase II of the case.

On 24 August 1994, U.S. District Court Chief Judge Murphy filed her Phase I decision: the Mille Lacs Band still had the right to fish, hunt and gather wild rice on public land under rules set by the Band.

Her decision meant that Indians would be allowed to net fish on Lake Mille Lacs. Non-Indians would be fined or arrested if they dared. Indians could spear fish out of the regular season. Spear-fishing was forbidden to everyone else.

The defendants asked for an injunction to prevent Band members from hunting and fishing under the Band's rules until after Phase II of the case. Murphy refused.

The State, counties and landowners vowed to appeal.

No One Was Listening

Did anyone in Congress notice what was going on in Minnesota? It didn't seem so. A federal court decision that went directly against the Fourteenth Amendment to the U.S. Constitution didn't seem to be of any importance in Washington, D.C. Only those involved in the case remained passionate about the issue, filing injunctions and appeals right away.

Perhaps because of her exemplary display of judicial activism, Judge Diana Murphy was rewarded with a promotion that moved her from the District Court to the Eighth Circuit Court of Appeals, the very Court that would be hearing the State's appeal of her lower-court decision.

The issues appealed included the following:

- Murphy's decision to uphold fishing, hunting and gathering privileges as described in the 1837 Treaty.

- Murphy's summary judgement limiting the number of legal arguments available to the State, counties, and landowners.
- Murphy's refusal to grant an injunction to prevent the Band from implementing the court's decision until completion of Phase II of the trial.

The Band submitted an 88-page fishing-and-hunting code that outlined its regulation plans for Lake Mille Lacs. The Code was similar to the one being used by the Wisconsin Chippewa. According to newspaper accounts, it did not leave out the possibility of commercial fishing.

Don Wedll, the Commissioner of Natural Resources for the Mille Lacs Band of Chippewa, had first said that if the Band won treaty fishing rights, it would limit itself to ceremonial harvests of fish, mostly by spearing. Eventually, he would admit to Dennis Anderson of the Minneapolis *Star Tribune* that, "Emphases have changed…now there may be an interest in a commercial harvest as well." Wedll assumed that the 1837 Treaty rights were a fact, and so the economic implications of the Band's taking up to fifty percent of the harvest were, in his opinion, beside the point. "…If the Mille Lacs band takes its share," he said, "there will be an impact on resorts…But no one says, 'Gee, we have been taking things we haven't had a right to take and exploiting them, for a long, long time,…' The bottom line is [non-Indians are] taking something that doesn't belong to them…. People aren't focusing on the fact that the Band has these rights, and people have built their businesses after taking those rights."

But non-Indian property owners in the Mille Lacs area had not "taken" any rights. They and their ancestors had purchased or been allotted the land. They had developed their businesses from nothing. They had paid, and were paying, state and local taxes.

Wedll ended by calling for "adjustments" because there were things done in the past that were not right. In other words, Minnesotans must be treated differently under the law in accordance to their race.

Phase II of the trial was scheduled for March of 1996. It would determine how much fish and game Band members would be entitled to. It was understood by everyone that it would be close to fifty percent, as had been the case in Wisconsin. Fifty percent of the fish harvest—a natural resource owned by all Minnesotans—given away to one percent of the State's population.

It was clear that the U.S. Supreme Court would eventually have to hear the case. All parties were prepared for the long journey to Washington, D.C. The Wisconsin case had taken seventeen years, and it had not even made it to the Supreme Court because the State of Wisconsin had decided not to seek certiorari. That was not going to happen in Minnesota.

Those displeased with Murphy's decision acted immediately. A few state senators indicated they would initiate legislation to end the Mille Lacs Band's gambling monopoly if the Band started fishing commercially. Native sovereignty nationalists countered that treaty rights were far more important to them than casinos. If it came to choosing between the two, treaty rights would come on top, always.

That seemed hard to believe.

Casino Fever — A Primer

By 1996, the American Indian gambling industry was a $6-billion-a-year cash cow. Casinos are increasingly associated with Native Americans. The Indian Gaming Regulatory Act of 1988

(25 U.S.C. § 2701-2721) allowed gaming by Indian tribes as a way to promote self-sufficiency, tribal economic development, and strong tribal governments. The Act coincided with a giant expansion in gambling in the United States. As of July of 1998, twenty-six states already had casinos and thirty-eight had lotteries. That same year, the Foxwoods Resort and Casino, in Mashantucket, Connecticut, was the most successful gambling hall in the world. Annual revenues totaled more than $1 billion.

Indian casinos have been so successful, in fact, that big battles have begun between tribes wishing to get in on the action and the states that oppose them. In California, forty-four tribes filed plans to expand casino gambling after voters in the state approved a measure to legalize certain gambling devices. The tribes spent more than $60 million in support of the measure during their campaign.

In April of 1997, Don Wedll, the Commissioner of Natural Resources for the Mille Lacs Band, said in an interview that the Band had received "tremendous" financial support from casino profits in their effort to assert their treaty privileges to fish, hunt and gather on the 1837 ceded territory.

Money Worries

Using the "racist" label was not enough to stop genuinely concerned citizens from appealing Judge Murphy's decision to uphold the Band's 1837 Treaty privileges. Supporters of the Band turned then to the question of money. The appeal would be extremely costly to Minnesota, they argued. Legal fees and administrative costs would grow, eventually totaling much more than the amount the tribe had sought in its original lawsuit. If the state legislature had passed the settlement, they said, paying the $8.6 million the Band had asked for, the state's taxpayers would not be burdened with mounting costs now.

A Minneapolis *Star Tribune* editorial commented: "The counties and landowners who have joined the suit on the state side seem content to piggyback on Minnesota's unlimited checkbook to carry their ignorant case."

Bud Grant replied: "Since when is advocating equal access under the same rules for all 'ignorant'?"

Band supporters were already predicting the outcome of the Eighth Circuit Court of Appeals decision and, if it went that far, the Supreme Court's, as well. Editorials opposed to the State were full of preemptive dismissal of the defendants' position. "Bud and his buddies are determined to take the case to the Supreme Court," one wrote. "They hold the cards, impossibly weak though their hand is."

Costs would certainly rise. Seven other bands of Chippewa had joined the Mille Lacs Band and the Department of Justice in the case. Six of them were Wisconsin Chippewa bands that had been party to the 1837 Treaty. The seventh was the Fond du Lac Band of Minnesota. They all claimed the same harvesting privileges.

It was going to cost dearly, indeed, to uphold the spirit of the Fourteenth Amendment to the U.S. Constitution, but no more than if Minnesota had given in to the demands of the tribe in the settlement negotiations. With the seven new bands joining the case, it was clear that a settlement would have done nothing to keep the tribes from suing again, and again, at any time in the future.

Phase II

Phase II of the case began in March of 1996. It would better define…

- where the treaty harvest could take place;
- how much of each species band members could harvest;
- which species could be harvested; and
- the harvesting methods to be allowed.

This phase of the trial seemed almost irrelevant since the outcome was as easy to guess as the outcome of Phase I. In mid-August, 1996, the Mille Lacs Band tried to get court approval to start exercising its fishing and hunting privileges before the conclusion of Phase II of the trial. The landowners and counties reacted with motions to stop approval, plus demands to unseal the Band's financial records. Secrecy in financial dealings with taxpayers' money is another perk of tribal governments. While everywhere in America, government finance is a matter of public record, "Indian Country" does not have to show anyone what it does with the money it receives from Uncle Sam.

Phase II of the trial eventually turned into a court-approved compromise.

Open Season

As expected, U.S. District Judge Michael Davis (overseeing Phase II) approved the Mille Lacs Band's conservation code. The Code included spear- and net-fishing of 40,000 pounds of Lake Mille Lacs walleye in the coming season, and it gave Indians longer harvesting seasons than non-Indians.

Davis also ruled, in January of 1997, that the Mille Lacs Band, as well as the Fond du Lac Band and the other Chippewa from Wisconsin, could begin their hunting and fishing according to the approved Code.

As a result, the Minnesota Department of Natural Resources (DNR) proposed to lower the allowable catch for non-Indians on

Lake Mille Lacs in order to accommodate the new harvest limit established by the Code. While the total limit for the lake would be set at 320,000 pounds of fish (much more than the 40,000 the Band was assigned), the Band's limit would increase in the coming years to fifty percent of the total.

But don't fret, supporters of treaty rights said. It was highly unlikely that the Band would ever take anything close to the limit allowed. What the bands really wanted, they said, was to make the point that the bands, not Minnesota, had the right to decide how tribal members harvested fish for subsistence.

Everyone knew, however, that subsistence was not the goal. Commercial fishing was. Band members had not depended on fish for survival in decades.

The DNR sought to delay the beginning of the tribes' harvesting season. The landowners and counties asked for an injunction to keep the Indians from fishing and hunting under their own code until the case went through its full course of appeals—to the U.S. Supreme Court, if necessary.

Judge Davis, following Diana Murphy's example, denied all requests for delays.

At the end of March of 1997, Governor Carlson requested air time from Minnesota radio and television stations to finally get visibly involved in the matter. His goal, he wrote, was to "avoid the kind of situation that erupted in Wisconsin in the late 1980s." The violent protests in Wisconsin had been the direct result of granting different treatment under the law to Wisconsin band members.

Part of Governor Carlson's request was to keep the media from sensationalizing the events that might take place once the bands began exercising their court-ordered special rights. "Many people are commenting that the media is looking for that story [about] one or two bad apples," Carlson's legal counsel, Tanja Kozicky, said.

Perhaps because of the fear of violence, the Eighth U.S. Circuit Court of Appeals saw the error in Judge Davis' stubbornness and stayed his order. This action delayed the start of fishing and hunting in the 1837 ceded territory under the bands' code until the Appeals Court itself reviewed the case and ruled on it.

In the meantime, the bands would be allowed to harvest 2,000 pounds of fish for ceremonial purposes only. This was a blow to the Chippewa since members had been getting ready to net and spear fish on twenty-nine lakes in the ceded territory.

To The Eighth Circuit

The Landowners

The Mille Lacs 1837 Treaty case was the first treaty-rights case in which landowners were allowed to intervene as defendants. Many citizens felt that Minnesota's Governor, Attorney General, and the DNR had not made much of an effort to defend equal treatment under the law for all state citizens. For that reason, the intervening property owners were seen as the key to winning the case.

Their participation was also a strategy: if the state or counties lost at the Eighth Circuit Court of Appeals level, and decided not to go on to the Supreme Court (as had happened in Wisconsin), the landowners would have the right to appeal on their own.

The landowners were John W. Thompson, Jenny Thompson, Joseph N. Karpen, LeRoy Burling, Glenn E. Thompson, and Gary M. Kiedrowski.

At the Eighth Circuit Court of Appeals, the landowners would concentrate on the following arguments:

- The 1850 Presidential Order extinguishing the fishing, hunting and gathering privileges of the Band;
- The 1855 Treaty;

- The Equal Footing Doctrine; and
- Payments made to the tribe by the Indian Claims Commission (ICC).

These were similar—except for the ICC payments—to the defenses the State had used at the district court level.

Judge Murphy had ruled that the 1850 Executive Order had been invalid because the Chippewa believed that their fishing privileges could be revoked by the President, as per the 1837 Treaty, only if tribal members "misbehaved." What the Chippewa had believed, in the district court's opinion, was more important than what the Treaty actually said.

The 1855 Treaty argument maintained that the Chippewa had ceded all rights, title and interest to all the tribe's lands in "the Territory of Minnesota or elsewhere."

There was an additional argument that could potentially be much more powerful and have a stronger effect on treaty-rights lawsuits across the country. That defense was the Equal Footing Doctrine, which rendered all treaty privileges temporary since, once a territory joined the Union as a state, on an "equal footing," all applicable treaties were supposed to be extinguished.

The Equal Footing Doctrine came out of the Northwest Ordinance of 1787, one of the acts passed by Congress under the Articles of Confederation. It guaranteed admittance of new states to the Union (after the original thirteen) under the same federal laws affecting the states that already existed. "Part of the authority granted to states when they enter the Union is regulation over much of their natural resources," said Scott Strand, the Assistant Attorney General of Minnesota.

The Eighth Circuit Court of Appeals

By the end of the nineteenth century, the Supreme Court was overwhelmed by the many cases it had to review on appeal from federal district courts. The solution was to create, on 3 March 1891, an intermediate level of appellate courts to filter the flow of cases. These were the Circuit Courts of Appeals.

Minnesota, Arkansas, Iowa, Missouri, Nebraska, North Dakota, and South Dakota were grouped into the Eighth of the twelve judicial circuits created for this new appeals level. Each circuit is assigned several Circuit Judges. Cases are usually heard by panels consisting of three of these judges. During the Mille Lacs case, the three-judge panel was composed of Donald P. Lay, John Gibson, and Theodore McMillian.

The hearing took place on 13 June 1997, in St. Paul, Minnesota. Each side was given forty minutes to present its position and arguments. Local interest in the case was such that the public filled two "overflow" rooms in addition to the actual courtroom. Those in the overflow section heard the case through an audio feed.

The arguments were familiar to everyone following the case by now. The bands insisted that the fishing, hunting and gathering privileges of the 1837 Treaty still existed. The defendants had several reasons for believing that the Treaty had been extinguished.

Beliefs, rather than facts, were also considered at the Circuit Court of Appeals. Judge Theodore McMillian questioned whether band members had understood the meaning of the treaty upon signing it. As the Minneapolis *Star Tribune* reported, what the Indians believed was "key, because courts have ruled that treaties must be construed as Indians understood them." The writer was referring, in part, to the 1942 *Tulee v. Washington* case, which had established this approach to Indian treaty cases.

The "beliefs" approach was yet another patronizing, belittling attitude toward the Chippewa. It implied that Indian negotiators at the time were too stupid to understand what was going on. Attorneys for the defendants argued that the language used had been plain and clear.

Ann Peterson, the Department of Justice attorney, disagreed: "That's clearly not the case with regard to Indian treaties."

Participants (& their attorneys)
Eighth Circuit Court of Appeals, June 13, 1997
St. Paul, Minnesota

Plaintiffs	Represented by
Mille Lacs Band of Chippewa	Marc D. Slonim of Seattle, Washington.
Fond du Lac Band of Chippewa	Douglas B. L. Endreson of Washington, D.C.
Seven Wisconsin bands of Chippewa	Ann Peterson of the U.S. Department of Justice.

Defendants	Represented by
State of Minnesota and Minnesota Department of Natural Resources	Peter Tester, Minnesota Assistant Attorney General
Nine Minnesota Counties	James Martin Johnson of Olympia, Washington
Six landowners	Stephen Froehle of Minneapolis, Minnesota

And the ruling is... "Good Law"

The three-judge panel filled sixty-three pages with its decision, but one sentence in it put it best: "Despite 160 years that have passed since the signing of the treaty, it remains good law." On 26 August 1997, the appeal was over.

According to the decision, the Chippewa still held the privilege to fish, hunt and gather in the 1837 ceded territory, under their own conservation code. Never mind what that meant to the Fourteenth Amendment to the U.S. Constitution, the three-judge panel implied. "One of the hallmarks of our constitutional system," Judge Donald P. Lay wrote, "is respect for the law, regardless of changing circumstances or the inevitable passage of time."

The decision included this twist: Indians would be fined if they didn't follow the rules of the state when fishing, hunting and gathering on private land in the ceded territory, even when the landowner had granted them permission to fish, hunt and gather on the property. This meant that the double standard had itself a double standard. DNR enforcement officers would have four classes of citizens to consider when it came to, say, net-fishing:

1. Indian on public property in ceded territory—legal.
2. Non-Indian on public property in ceded territory—illegal.
3. Indian on private property in ceded territory—illegal.
4. Non-Indian on private property in ceded territory—illegal.

There seemed to be no bounds to how ridiculous judicial activism could become.

Rod Sando, the Minnesota DNR Commissioner, tried to make light of the whole thing by saying afterwards that the decision meant "a new beginning of resource management in east-central Minnesota rather than an end....It is not a resource defeat. I have no doubt that our children and grandchildren will be able to have the same outdoor experiences that you and I enjoy." But that wasn't true. From now on, Indians and non-Indians would certainly have *different* experiences. Two groups of U.S. citizens treated differently under "Good Law."

Marge Anderson, the Chief Executive of the Mille Lacs Band of Chippewa was pleased. "After seven years of struggling to reestablish our treaty rights," she said, "we feel vindicated by the court's ruling."

Governor Arne Carlson vowed to appeal the decision.

Howard Hanson, the Minneapolis businessman, noted that it was "a sad day for the citizens of Minnesota and a sad day for the Constitution. We knew," he said, "the day this case was filed that it was going to the Supreme Court, and it will."

The Mille Lacs Advisory Association, representing some seventy property owners and businesses on the lake, said it would issue a response about the ruling after holding a meeting. Eddy Lyback, its president, said, "I hope the state and the landowners continue with the appeals process."

Legal bills for the landowners had mounted to $900,000 already. The State had spent about $2.5 million. It was not made public how much the nine counties had spent, nor the bands of Chippewa and their chief supporter, the U.S. Department of Justice.

Aftermath of The Eighth

The Wisconsin and Minnesota bands of Chippewa would not be able to begin fishing, hunting and gathering under their own code until mid-October, 1997, when the stay expired. Scott Strand, the Minnesota Assistant Attorney General, said that either the state, the counties or landowners would seek another stay, if not from the Eighth Circuit Court, then from the U.S. Supreme Court.

In the meantime, the Minnesota Department of Natural Resources was getting ready to "cross-deputize" its officers with tribal conservation officers so that both could enforce the separate set of hunting and fishing rules. Non-Indians accused of infractions would go to state court. Band members to tribal court, which was believed to be much more lenient.

You Be The Judge

Say you are an avid sportsman and one day go fishing with a good friend of yours. Your friend happens to be a band member. You are not. All of a sudden, DNR enforcement agents show up. You and your friend have been having a good time—talking, drinking a few beers—unaware of passing your catch limit. Both you and your friend must appear in court. You are sent to state court. He goes to tribal court. A few days later, you talk to your friend and find out that he was treated differently under tribal law than you were under state law. He got off with a warning. You paid a fine.

Once the fishing began in October of 1997, the bands would be entitled to 40,000 pounds of Mille Lacs walleye, with the Mille Lacs Band getting half of that. The other seven bands would share the remaining 20,000 pounds. The following year, the bands' quota was expected to rise to 55,000 pounds.

Again, supporters of treaty rights insisted that fears about band members exhausting the available supply of fish had no basis. James Mitchell, a Mille Lacs member, noted that fishing wasn't a big thing for the Band. "How many Indians do you see on the lake?" he said. "They don't buy boats. They're really not into this recreation stuff. We don't go out there for a daily diet."

On the hunting side, the DNR cut the number of antlerless deer permits issued to non-Indians by ten percent, to compensate for the allocation of deer to band members, who would also enjoy a longer deer season (from the beginning of September to the end of December) when hunting with firearms. In addition, they would be allowed to "shine" deer with spotlights during a hunt, a practice that was illegal for everyone else.

As reported by the *Star Tribune*, the federal government had negotiated a separate agreement with the bands regarding waterfowl in 1985. Duck and goose hunters, if they were Indian, could take a higher daily limit than non-Indians under the agreement. It was not clear who had given the federal government the right to give away state natural resources to only a small number of Minnesota citizens.

It is important to remember that the 1837 Treaty case was never about Indians not being allowed to fish or hunt. They had the right to do so all along. They were allowed the same bag limits as anyone else, the same number of fish per person, the same methods. Their hunting and fishing seasons started and ended on the same dates as for all other citizens.

The Next Step — Lifting the Stay

Eager to Start Fishing

By 5 September 1997, newspapers were reporting that the Mille Lacs Band of Chippewa wanted the Eighth Circuit Court to lift the stay so that members could begin hunting and fishing immediately under their own code. They did not want to wait until mid-October.

But they had to—until October 20, in fact—when the Federal Appeals Court gave the go ahead. Jim Genia, the attorney representing the Mille Lacs Band in the case, said that members would be "out hunting deer and possibly fishing within a few days."

Then the Eighth Circuit Court came out with the most extraordinary statement. Its reason for lifting the stay, it said, was that there existed "no likelihood of success" for the state to win an appeal, thus preempting the result of what the U.S. Supreme Court might decide if it agreed to hear the case.

Although the State had asked that the case be heard by the full Eighth Circuit Court (that is, all the judges of the Court instead of the three-judge panel that had ruled in August), it was obvious that the petition would be denied.

And it was, in November of 1997. The vote was 7 to 2 against reviewing the August ruling by the three-judge panel. All that was left for the state, counties and landowners was the U.S. Supreme Court.

Immediately, Band supporters started gloating at the fact that it would be next to impossible to get the U.S. Supreme Court to hear the case. The highest court of the land receives approximately 7,000 petitions to hear cases every year, but grants hearings to only about 80 of them.

Private Lands, Too

While the bands had said they didn't want any privileges on private land—and the Eighth Circuit Court's decision had explicitly ruled that band members did not have treaty privileges on private land in the ceded territory—Mark and Debra Zebroski of Brainerd, Minnesota, received a letter from the DNR soon after the full Eighth Circuit Court of Appeals refused to review the case.

The letter contradicts both what the Band had said and the Court's ruling. "County records indicate you own lands under the Tree Growth Law..." wrote Rod Sando, the DNR Commissioner, to the Zebroskis. "This letter is to advise you that Indian Band members may be using these lands subject to the Band codes..."

DNR Signs Agreement

DNR Commissioner Sando went on to sign an agreement with the Chippewa bands that would raise their 1998 walleye limit to 55,000 pounds (from 40,000 the previous year), and up to 100,000 pounds by the year 2002.

In the Spring of 1998, David Smith, Jr., a Band member, used nets to catch walleye. "You can do it legally now instead of going out at three or four in the morning," he said, not mentioning the fact that it was still illegal for ninety-nine percent of the state's population. He could do it because he considered it his birthright and the courts had so far agreed. This idea of birthright and heritage, rather than equal treatment under the law, persisted in the view of treaty-rights supporters. "I think most tribal members are thankful they are finally able to do things their grandparents told them they had the right to do," Don Wedll, the Band's Commissioner of Natural Resources, said.

Supreme Court: Last Stop

After the U.S. Supreme Court was asked in February of 1998 to review the case, treaty-rights supporters continued to downplay the chances that the petition would be granted. Jim Genia, attorney for the Mille Lacs, said there were no novel legal issues left for the Supreme Court to consider. "There's a long line of federal decisions upholding these [treaty] rights," he said. That "long line" was not taken seriously, however, especially when several court rulings were believed by many to be the result of judicial activism more than the upholding of the rule of law.

Peter Tester, representing the State of Minnesota, was confident that the Supreme Court would agree to review the case because the Eighth Circuit Court of Appeals had not followed Supreme Court precedent. In fact, several appeals courts in the country had been giving contradictory rulings regarding treaty rights. That meant it was the right time for the highest court of the land to step in and settle the matter once and for all.

The best example that the U.S. Supreme Court was indeed interested in cases dealing with Indian rights came just a few days later, when the high court decided the *Leech Lake Band of Chippewa Indians v. Cass County, Minn.*, another case about treating Minnesota citizens differently under the law. The federal government had also been on the side of the tribe in this case, as had been the National Congress of American Indians and several Chippewa bands in Minnesota.

In the *Leech Lake* case, Cass County had been sued for taxing twenty-one parcels of land that the Band had purchased from non-Indians. The Band claimed the land was exempt from property taxes because it had once been part of a reservation and thus non-taxable. The case had followed these steps:

1. The district court had ruled that the land was taxable.
2. The Eighth Circuit Court of Appeals had decided that only thirteen out of the twenty-one parcels were taxable.
3. The Supreme Court had now ruled that the remaining eight parcels were also subject to property taxes, no matter who owned them.

In this case, the Band's lawsuit had backfired, not only because the tribe lost the case in the end, but because it made very public the scheme being perpetrated by tribes and the federal government all over the country. The scheme was simple: a tribe bought private land (increasingly with casino profits) and immediately tried to place it in trust status with the federal government, taking it out of state jurisdiction and off local tax rolls in the process.

You Be The Judge

You own a beautiful home on five acres. The property has been in your family for three generations. Since it is near a large metropolitan area, convenient to a state highway, property taxes on it have gone up steadily in the last few years. Your children are all away in college. You can't afford the taxes on your four-bedroom home anymore, and see yourself forced to sell the place.

> The buyer turns out to be a tribe, which immediately files a lawsuit claiming that the property qualifies for trust status because it was once on tribal land. The result: the tribe doesn't have to pay property taxes on it—the main reason you were forced to sell the house in the first place.

Thirteen states and ten other Minnesota counties had supported Cass County in the case. So had the National Governors Association, the National League of Cities, the U.S. Conference of Mayors, and the Council of State Governments.

Nervous Reaction: Cocky Comments

The prospect that the U.S. Supreme Court might actually grant certiorari on the Mille Lacs case started to make treaty-rights proponents nervous. The evidence was in the editorials and articles they wrote. Their arguments centered on the fact that the lower courts had already decided the case. "The lower courts," went one editorial in *The Minnesota Daily*, "fully support the Chippewa and U.S. government claims that the treaty is still valid."

But the role of courts is not to "support" anything but to correctly interpret the law.

"Since 1990," the writer continued, "Minnesota and its co-plaintiffs have been spending millions to present their case in different courts. They lost each time....Based on the history of the case, the treaty's opponents don't deserve another hearing."

It takes a lot of fear to so sweepingly dismiss people's rights to pursue constitutional justice at the highest level of appeal. What else if not fear would drive anyone to declare that a case doesn't "deserve" a hearing in the U.S. Supreme Court?

Treaty-rights champions continued to talk and write about how much more fish non-Indians would still get over Indians even when the 1837 Treaty stood. They did not seem to understand (or admit that they understood) that the case was not only about sharing a few fish but about following the blueprint responsible for social stability in the United States of America—the idea that all citizens must be treated equally under the law.

More Restrictions

In March of 1998 the Minnesota Department of Natural Resources announced that Lake Mille Lacs anglers (i.e., mostly non-Indians) would face lower limits on northern pike due to treaty rights affecting the species. Tribal nets meant for walleye would inevitably catch some northern pike, so the non-Indian limit on that species had to be adjusted.

Even the combined "safe harvest" limit for Mille Lacs walleye had been decreased by the DNR for 1998, from 320,000 pounds the previous year to 260,000 pounds.

The announcement itself was expected to affect the resort industry in the Mille Lacs area. Once the lower limit took effect, sportsmen would make plans to fish other lakes that had fewer restrictions. Why spend money on Mille Lacs if you couldn't fish? This was the perception, even if it was still possible to fish as much as in previous years. News stories about restrictions would be enough to keep people away.

In the meantime, the Band was still trying to redefine the Mille Lacs Indian "Reservation" as an actual reservation covering 61,000 acres. And the U.S. Environmental Protection Agency (EPA) was giving it a hand through its Underground Injection Control Program (UICP).

The UICP is a sewage treatment program administered for the EPA by state authorities. Instead of designating state officials as overseers of the local UICP, the EPA designated tribal officials as having "primacy," thus implying that there still was a 61,000-acre Mille Lacs Reservation.

Involvement by federal agencies in state affairs by using Indian tribes as pawns goes back to John Collier's time. The idea has always been to take away state jurisdiction from state land and transfer it to the federal government by placing such land in trust status for the Indians. Trust status simply means that the tribes own the land but can never have full control over it because Indians are wards of the federal government and Congress decides what is to be done with their land.

Collier's goal was to save "our vanishing resources," as he put it, and the "Indian folk-life."

"On October 25, 1937," he wrote in *From Every Zenith*, "I incorporated the Resources Board's findings into an administrative order....Secretary [of the Interior, Harold L.] Ickes approved my order....whose full text may be found in *The Living Wilderness* of December, 1937, and again in *The Living Wilderness* of July, 1940."

The administrative order called for setting aside "sixteen Indian areas which...were decreed to remain roadless until such time as the order might be modified." The purpose was to "save for the Nation some fragments of commercially un-exploited wilderness."

A trend had been set: Indians as pawns of the government.

Sovereign Immunity

While Minnesota awaited certiorari from the U.S. Supreme Court, Senator Slade Gorton (Washington State) introduced a bill to curtail Native American "sovereign immunity."

Sovereign immunity is the concept used by the tribes to "shield themselves from lawsuits and accountability in state district court where the mandates of state and federal constitutions apply," wrote Judge R. A. Randall, of the Minnesota Court of Appeals, in an opinion.

The tribes didn't like the idea of being sued, but they were eager to exercise their rights to sue others. As the landowners' petition for certiorari in the U.S. Supreme Court stated, "If the Petition is denied, tribes will be able to pick state defendants, and commence a new round of litigation...."

The citizens of Minnesota were eagerly awaiting the high Court's decision to hear the case.

Certiorari

The case that, according to critics, didn't deserve a day in the U.S. Supreme Court, was granted certiorari on 8 June 1998. The hearing would take place in the fall, with a decision announced in 1999.

Marge Anderson, the Mille Lacs Band Chief Executive, informed the public that "The lower courts have repeatedly affirmed our rights, and we are confident the U.S. Supreme Court will do the same."

Bud Grant was pleased that the case was finally going to be heard in a court less susceptible to outside pressures. "Money won't affect the Supreme Court," he said. "Now [the case] is out of the political arena and out of the money arena....we're on a level-playing field."

Governor Arne Carlson said that Minnesota would now be able to "vigorously fight for state control of Lake Mille Lacs."

Strategy

Attorneys for both sides set to work on their briefs. The State of Minnesota, counties and landowners had now become the

Petitioners for the Supreme Court hearing. The Band and the Federal Government had become the Respondents.*

Attorney Malcolm MacGregor, of the firm Persian, MacGregor and Thompson, had three principal arguments to present on behalf of the landowners. They were the 1850 Presidential Order, the 1855 Treaty, and the Equal Footing Doctrine. These didn't differ from the appeal at the Eighth Circuit Court level, but they would be given more force with Supreme Court precedents such as the 1985 *Oregon Department of Fish and Wildlife et al. v. Klamath Indian Tribe.* In the Klamath case, the tribe had filed a claim against the State of Oregon's Department of Fish and Wildlife for "interfering with the fishing rights of members" fishing on lands ceded through a 1901 agreement. The Court had ruled for the State of Oregon.

Another argument Persian, MacGregor and Thompson had in representing the landowners was one of jurisdiction: Indian Claims Commission payments had been made to the band regarding the 1837 ceded territory. As a result, courts of law had no jurisdiction in the case, and the lower courts should have never considered the Band's lawsuit. As had been the case earlier, this argument would end up being ignored.

Odd Behavior — Minnesota Nice

Because of widespread interest in the case by several states that could be affected by Indian treaty claims, there was a rush of filings of friend-of-the-court briefs. One of these *Amicus Curiae* briefs, as they are known, was filed for the Citizens Equal Rights Alliance (CERA) in support of the Petitioners.

** This is a simplification. The U.S. Supreme Court has a confusing way of grouping participating parties, calling the landowners "Respondents," as if they were on the same side of the Mille Lacs Band of Chippewa, in this case.*

When Amicus briefs are submitted, all parties in the suit must approve them—and they almost always do. In this case, however, the State of Minnesota refused to accept CERA's brief, even when it supported the state's position.

"One wonders why the state would do this," Lana E. Marcussen, co-author of the brief, said. "It's almost as if the Attorney General doesn't want to do everything he can to win this case."

Jim Johnson, the attorney for the counties in the case, was also puzzled. "Minnesota's refusal to accept an Amicus is not supported by any public policy position I've ever heard of," he said.

This seemed to indicate that state politicians were regretting their move to appeal to the Supreme Court, and that the strength of the appeal might have to depend on the counties and landowners from now on. It wasn't surprising: State officials had also refused to use the Indian Claims Commission argument in the case, an argument that the landowners believed was the most likely to succeed.

Julie Shortridge, a free-lance reporter for *The Native American Press/Ojibwe News* (and now the paper's editor) offered a possible explanation: "Attorney General Skip Humphrey is running for Minnesota Governor, and is the current front-runner in receiving DFL [Democratic-Farm-Labor, as the Democrats are known in Minnesota] endorsement. DFL candidates in Minnesota typically count tribal governments among their most generous supporters."

Skip Humphrey—son of the late Hubert Humphrey, Vice President under Lyndon Johnson—had also refused to submit Amicus briefs in two other tribal-related cases that were pending before the Supreme Court, according to Shortridge.

Humphrey would eventually lose the governorship to Jesse Ventura, of the Reform Party.

In the end, all parties to the case consented. Marcussen and co-counsel Brian A. Thomas got to file their Amicus brief for the Citizens Equal Rights Alliance.

"CERA's interest in this lawsuit," the brief explains, "arises from CERA's advocacy of the principle that all people should be treated equally, whether Indian or non-Indian. In this, CERA's interest mirrors that of Petitioners. The Chippewa Bands' position that they are entitled to the reinstatement of treaty rights to avoid application of state police power authority to regulate hunting, fishing, and gathering rights applicable to all other state citizens, violates the principle of equal rights under the law."

"Runners Needed"

The U.S. Supreme Court hearing was set for 2 December 1998. As the date approached, Native sovereignty nationalists organized their public relations machine and professional lobbyists. The Midwest Treaty Network's Internet site announced the organizing of the *Waabanong Spiritual Run* to "take the Treaty Staff from Lac du Flambeau, Wisconsin, to Washington, D.C., in time for the Dec. 2 hearing."

The Treaty Staff—a ceremonial pole or club—had come to the Ojibwe in Wisconsin "during their treaty struggles in the mid-1980s," the Network explained. It was "intended to be used by Ojibwe tribes in treaty litigation to bring about a positive outcome." Relay runners were to take it from November 11 on to the end of the month, when they were expected to reach Washington, D.C., where a Sacred Fire would be lit to burn until the day of the hearing.

"We are in need of core team runners,..." the Network announced, "to commit to the entire relay run." People willing to help with money, food, shelter, or anything else, were asked to contact the Great Lakes Indian Fish and Wildlife Commission (GLIFWC) office.

The Network did a good job at clearly defining what was at stake for the tribe. This case had to do with the Minnesota Ojibwe, it said, but "findings could potentially impact the treaty rights of Wisconsin tribes and tribes nationally....TREATY RIGHTS OF ALL TRIBES AT RISK!"

An adverse decision on the Mille Lacs case based...

- on the 1855 Treaty, would only affect the Mille Lacs Band;
- on the 1850 Presidential Order, would affect other Ojibwe bands, as well; and
- on the Equal Footing Doctrine, would affect treaty rights across the country.

The Waabanong Run was to go through the states of Wisconsin, Illinois, Indiana, Ohio, West Virginia, Pennsylvania, Maryland, and the District of Columbia.

The Network even posted a day-to-day journal of what the participants were experiencing as they approached the nation's capital. The journals contained a painstaking amount of detail. Activities included praying for Supreme Court Justice Sandra Day O'Connor and her family (Day 3), Chief Justice Rehnquist (Day 4), Justice Antonin Scalia (Day 5), Justice John Paul Stevens (Day 6), Justice Clarence Thomas and his family (Day 9), etc.—plus smoking pipes, "smudging" runners, holding interviews with TV and radio stations, suffering assorted running injuries, enjoying a sweat lodge, and generally having a good time.

But they never forgot the public relations purpose of the run. On Day 7, they reported: "Several policemen stopped and inquired in a friendly manner about what we were doing. We gave them a copy of our press release and one said he'd pass it 'down the line.'"

In addition, the National Congress of American Indians (NCAI) passed a resolution…

- declaring 2 December 1998, "Spirit of Treaties Day for Indian nations," and asking for "spiritual support from Indian communities across the nation as Ojibwe treaty rights go on trial;"
- supporting the "spiritual run with the Treaty Staff from Lac du Flambeau, Wisconsin, to Washington, D.C., as a demonstration of deep concern regarding the preservation of tribally held treaty rights in the United States;" and
- announcing its intention to "help coordinate tribal, spiritual ceremonies in Washington, D.C., on December 2, 1998, in recognition of [the] importance of retaining the rights and sacredness of the treaty rights which our Indian forefathers preserved for our generation and generations to come."

Supreme Court Hearing

Sacred Fire

Smoke rose from the Sacred Fire during the four days before the hearing. It symbolized, according to participants, Native American prayers going up.

Despite NCAI's resolution, the Waabanong Run, and all the public relations efforts to stir the Native American community with "All Tribes at Risk!" warnings, there were surprisingly few people representing Indian tribes at the hearing. By November 25, the Midwest Treaty Network's Internet site had been visited a mere 381 times (it claimed 900 visits a few days later).

The interest just didn't seem to be there. Of the estimated two million-plus American Indians in the United States, an unexpectedly small number of them had shown up. The low turnout seemed to indicate that most enrolled members prefer to be treated the same as any American citizen. This may also be the reason why more than seventy-five percent of Native Americans don't even live on reservations.

The Mille Lacs 1837 Treaty case was given docket number 97-1337 at the U.S. Supreme Court. Critics had said it couldn't be done. But here they were—the state, the counties, and the landowners—having their appeal heard by the highest court of the land on 2 December 1998.

Tradition

Before a hearing starts, decorum and quiet reign in the Court. (A man reading a pocket novel during the waiting period was brusquely told by a court employee to "put that away!") The atmosphere in the Court is that of a secret society's initiation rite, of respect for respect itself—the sort of thing we see less and less of in public life today.

The public stands when the justices appear. It all seems alien and pompous, pure Hollywood. In the book *The Benchwarmers*, Joseph Goulden explains: "The formal trappings of the judiciary remind the judge daily of his importance. The stage-setting of a federal courtroom is intended to give an aura of high dignity to whatever happens there."

The black robes are part of the symbolism. Goulden calls them "a hand-me-down from the English monarchy that American public opinion does not permit to be draped across the carcass of any political official…."

But there is a purpose to the robes other than to impress the public. "Judges should be clothed in robes," Chief Justice William Howard Taft said once, "not only that those who witness the administration of justice should be properly advised that the function performed is one different from, and higher than, that which a man discharges as a citizen in the ordinary walks of life, but also, in order to impress the judge himself with constant consciousness that he is a high priest in the temple of justice."

H. L. Mencken had a more secular view of such high priests of justice: "A judge is a law student who corrects his own papers."

The Supreme Court's "Visitor's Guide to Oral Argument," which is given to all attendees, states that "Notetaking is not permitted. Sunglasses, identification tags (other than military), display buttons and inappropriate clothing may not be worn" in the courtroom. The Guide offers no definition of what inappropriate clothing is. But in today's America, it is widely understood that going to the Supreme Court is as serious as going to an important job interview. A suit, if not a tie, would show respect and interest in the proceedings.

A way for Native sovereignty nationalists to rebel against the current system of law is to ignore the Supreme Court's dress code. This is not to say that they showed up in Native American regalia at the Mille Lacs hearing. Instead, some of them wore tee-shirts, jeans, and sneakers—grown adults looking like disheveled teenagers. Of course, sovereignty nationalists will claim that the U.S. Supreme Court is not *their* court, so they have no duty to respect its rules. But respect for other cultures goes both ways. It looked as if those few at the hearing were in need of some sensitivity training.

No one was kicked out (the world would have heard about it), and one had to wonder what would happen to a scruffy white man, in a tee shirt and sneakers, if he showed up to a hearing, alone, in an unrelated case.

U.S. Supreme Court Justices

Chief Justice **William H. Rehnquist** (appointed by President Nixon, 1972; elevated to Chief Justice by President Reagan, 1986); **John Paul Stevens** (Ford, 1975); **Sandra Day O'Connor** (Reagan, 1981); **Antonin Scalia** (Reagan, 1986); **Anthony M. Kennedy** (Reagan, 1988); **David H. Souter** (Bush, 1990); **Clarence Thomas** (Bush, 1991); **Ruth Bader Ginsburg** (Clinton, 1993); **Stephen G. Breyer** (Clinton, 1994).

Supreme Court Procedures

The Supreme Court begins its terms on the first Monday of October. The terms last through June of the following year. Annually, from 70 to 100 cases are heard (the total has decreased in recent years).

During a term, the Court usually hears oral arguments two weeks out of each month. There are three or four one-hour arguments a day, three days a week. Depending on the case, individual attorneys get from ten to thirty minutes to present their arguments.

Path to the Supreme Court

The two most common ways for civil cases to reach the Court are:

1. The case is first filed in a **State Court**.
   It is appealed to the **State Supreme Court**.
   It is appealed to the **U.S. Supreme Court**.*

2. The case is first filed in **Federal District Court**.
   It is appealed to the **Circuit Court of Appeals.**
   It is appealed to the **U.S. Supreme Court**.*

* Technically, cases are not appealed to the Supreme Court because appeals are not automatic. The losing party must first seek certiorari. Unlike lower courts, the Supreme Court can choose not to hear a case.

Let's Hear It

Those attending a U.S. Supreme Court hearing for the first time are often startled by the apparent rudeness of the justices. The attorneys—who have spent endless hours preparing for the event—have little chance to direct their own presentations. John Kirwin, Assistant Attorney General of Minnesota, the first to step before the justices, was interrupted less than a minute into his argument with what at first seemed unrelated questions to what he had been talking about.

The justices had read the briefs and didn't want to deal with background information on the case. They wanted to clarify the details by asking direct questions. The attorneys representing the petitioners and respondents were there to answer those questions, nothing else.

At The U.S. Supreme Court, Washington, D.C.

Minnesota, et al., Petitioners v.
Mille Lacs Band of Chippewa Indians, et al.
(a.k.a. Mille Lacs 1837 Treaty Case)
Docket # 97-1337 December 2, 1998

On behalf of the Petitioners:

- John L. Kirwin, Esq., Assistant Attorney General of Minnesota, St. Paul, Minnesota.
- Randy V. Thompson, Esq., (Persian, MacGregor & Thompson) Minneapolis, Minnesota, representing the landowners.

On behalf of the Respondents

- Marc D. Slonim, Esq., Seattle, Washington.
- Barbara B. McDowell, Esq., Assistant to the Solicitor General, Department of Justice, Washington, D.C.

Both sides were prepared to argue about the 1850 Executive Order, the 1855 Treaty, and the Equal Footing Doctrine—and how all three affected the 1837 Treaty one way or another. But most of the questions from the justices centered on the 1850 Executive Order, which reads:

> The privileges granted temporarily to the Chippewa Indians of the Mississippi, by the Fifth Article of the Treaty made with them on the 29th of July 1837 "of hunting, fishing and gathering the wild rice, upon the lands, the rivers and the lakes included in the territory ceded" by that treaty to the United States; and the right granted to the Chippewa Indians of the Mississippi and Lake Superior, by the Second Article of the treaty with them of October 4th 1842, of hunting on the territory which they ceded by that treaty, "with the other usual privileges of occupancy until required to remove by the President of the United States," are hereby revoked; and all of the said Indians remaining on the lands ceded as aforesaid, are required to remove to their unceded lands. — Z. Taylor. Executive Office.
>
> Washington City, February 6th, 1850.
>
> By the President. I. Ewing, Secretary of the Interior.

How did the Chippewa and the Department of Justice view the 1850 Executive Order?

- It had been "abandoned...before it took effect." Only Executive Orders that are enforced or followed through are valid.
- It did not follow the general law of executive orders and had to therefore be put in the context of the 1837 Treaty.
- It had the purpose of removing the Indians and revoking their hunting and fishing rights. Since the government

failed to remove the Indians, the revocation part of the Order never took effect.

- It was not valid because lower courts had said so.
- Invalid because the Indians had been told that it had been an "order to remove." They had never been told that it meant they could no longer hunt or fish.

Article 5 of the 1837 Treaty contained the wording "during the pleasure of the President of the United States" as the duration of the fishing, hunting and gathering privileges of the tribe. The contemporary Chippewa and the Department of Justice (Respondents) believed that…

- the bands had not understood the meaning of "pleasure of the president" at the time of signing the treaty. They thought there had to be a cause for revocation and removal. Since there was no cause, the 1850 Executive Order was invalid.
- pleasure of the president meant the president could go back and forth: Now you can fish and hunt; now you can't; now you can. It was up to the President.
- the President could not end the fishing, hunting and gathering privileges unless he was "displeased with the Indians." That was what pleasure of the president had meant to the bands.

To the State of Minnesota, counties, and landowners (Petitioners)…

- "pleasure of the President" meant that the President had the right to revoke the hunting and fishing privileges and not to reinstate them. Once revoked, they were revoked for good. Only Congress could reinstate them.

Were The 1837 Treaty Privileges Still Active?

Respondents' view:

- If there are ambiguities in the language of a treaty, they should be resolved in favor of the Indians.

Petitioners' view:

- "There is certainly a significant encroachment on the State's ability to regulate" fishing and hunting (on public lands) under the lower courts' decisions.
- When the Chippewa ceded "all right, title, and interest to the land," any rights to hunt and fish on the ceded land were terminated.
- When a tribe receives compensation from the Indian Claims Commission and no deduction is mentioned as payment for maintaining fishing and hunting privileges, then the compensation received includes hunting and fishing rights, too.
- The language used in the 1837 Treaty was that of typical real estate conveyance, meaning all rights were conveyed with the ceded land.

One subject brought up by the Respondents was the issue of cultural survival, which in their view covered the following points:

- The Mille Lacs Band needs to fish and hunt its own way in order to save its dying culture.
- Treaty harvesting privileges still "put food on their tables and are central to their culture."
- Indians cannot hunt and fish under the same regulations that apply to non-Indians (i.e., with a state license) because cultural activities occur out of season and require

practices—like spear-fishing in the spring spawning season—that are illegal.

- Fish have to be caught with a spear, or it won't be traditional.
- Indians cannot feed their families if they have to follow state laws. Hunting, fishing, and gathering wild foods help "pay for life's necessities."

No one brought up the Mille Lacs Band's 1998 gross revenue from its two northern Minnesota casinos: $200 million. How can a band with that kind of income and merely 3,000 members not feed itself?

Even Band members like Frank Boyd, the transportation director for the Band's schools, admitted that the case had nothing to do with culture or survival. "I don't need to go out with a rifle and shoot all the deer I want," he said. "But I want to know the right is there. If it was there before Minnesota was here as a state, why should Minnesota be able to dictate to us?"

Wouldn't we all want to say things like that? If no Sixteenth Amendment existed before 1913, why should the IRS be able to dictate to us every April 15?

A Few Laughs

Barbara McDowell's turn in front of the bench was the most interesting and lively part of the hearing. She was the last one to stand before the justices and, as assistant to the Solicitor General, she was expected to come up with a powerful argument. When she was called, she smiled to the audience on her way to the lectern, as if about to receive an award.

Her perkiness came to an abrupt stop when she argued that "it was clear as time went on over the…four-year period after the [executive] order was issued, that the President…did not want the Chippewa to be removed." Chief Justice Rehnquist said, "Well, President Taylor died in 1850…so he didn't continue to think about it for four years."

McDowell seemed not so much unprepared but lacking any historical or legal basis that would allow her to argue a strong case. When the question of President Franklin Roosevelt's 1938 letter—asserting that the Chippewa's right to hunt and fish had ended—came up, McDowell said that "President Roosevelt's statement is entitled to a certain amount of deference, but he was not entirely informed about the situation."

That reply infuriated some justices, especially since President Roosevelt's letter emphasized the fact that he had indeed been informed.

Referring to the Chippewa who had ceded land in areas of Michigan and Wisconsin, Roosevelt wrote: "Indians of the Bad River Reservation now have no greater right to hunt or fish on the ceded area within which their reservation is located than do the other citizens of the State. Therefore, the Indians who hunt or fish or who have fish and game in their possession outside of their reservation or on lands under the jurisdiction of the State within their reservation are amenable to the State game laws and are subject to arrest and conviction for violation thereof."

The irony was that Roosevelt's administration had been one of the most useful to Indian sovereignty nationalists in the twentieth century. Under the Indian New Deal, the Indian Reorganization Act had been passed, and John Collier had enjoyed the freedom to push his separatist agenda.

When the hour was up, no one had been given the chance to discuss the Equal Footing Doctrine, an indication that the Court might base its decision on the 1850 Executive Order alone, which would not do much for supporting the Fourteenth Amendment anywhere in the country other than on the 1837 ceded territory.

Fresh Air

Outside, it was one of the most beautiful fall days so far that year. All parties, their supporters and opponents gathered in front of the Court.

The media were ready with their cameras and microphones to fill air time and newsprint with the participants' reactions. While the more visible supporters and opponents of the case were being interviewed, the American flag outside the Court was curiously flying upside down, attached to the staff only at its lower left corner. Coincidence? Title 36 (U.S.C. § 176(a)) states that "The flag should never be displayed with the union down, except as a signal of dire distress in instances of extreme danger to life or property." Upside-down American flags were also used prominently by American Indian Movement activists in the 1970s.

Perhaps it was fear of losing the case that made a few Native sovereignty nationalists behave so rudely during the interviews, interrupting and yelling while opponents talked to the cameras. It is reprehensible that a few bad apples in the Indian community encourage a stereotype of "Indian rudeness," instead of reflecting the values of respect for others' opinions shared by most Native Americans.

The bad apples kept on yelling, "My rights, not yours!" While Fourteenth Amendment supporter Howard Hanson was being interviewed, his voice could hardly be heard away from the microphone due to the yelling going on around him. "Liar, racist!" The bad apples wouldn't let him talk. "My rights, not yours!"

The same happened to Ray Stawski, a member of the Hunting and Angling Club, who read a prepared statement denouncing the racist stereotyping and divisiveness that the treaty case had generated. Stawski had taken his nine-year-old daughter to the hearing to show her that whole communities should not be judged by the actions of a few.

Along with the loud heckling, the term "timber niggers" was being bandied about—by Indians themselves. The mantra went something like this: "They are all racists [the equal-treatment-under-the-law supporters]. They call us timber niggers. They call us timber niggers. They call us timber niggers." In fact, no one was calling Native Americans anything. The only ones there using the racist epithet were the sovereignty nationalists. Many of the non-Indians present had never heard the term.

Curiously, the rudeness and racist remarks did not make the news, as they had in Wisconsin, where it had been non-Indians being rude and racist at the boat-landing protests.

After Hanson and others, it was time for supporters of different treatment based on race to express their views to the media. No one yelled anything then. Tom Maulson, Chairman of the Lac du Flambeau Band of Wisconsin, was allowed to speak his mind without interruption. So was longtime AIM activist Vernon Bellecourt.

There were several members of Wisconsin bands present because of the potential effect a loss in the Mille Lacs case might have on them. Wisconsin bands had been exercising their 1837 privilege to hunt and fish for more than a decade. If the Supreme Court reversed the Eighth Circuit Court of Appeals' decision now, it would open the door to efforts to reverse the Seventh Circuit Court of Appeals' ruling (the one that applied to Wisconsin). After the way the Supreme Court hearing had gone, the Wisconsin bands probably feared such a thing might happen.

My Race is More Ethnic Than Yours

The Handy Epithet

"As long as the government advocates preferential treatment for any group, they're advocating racism," said David Bentley, the manager of a resort on Lake Mille Lacs.

Race was an issue in the Mille Lacs case from the very beginning, not because it had anything to do with it but because the call of "racism" seems to be the handiest tool available to silence opponents when someone doesn't like what they are saying.

Consider the following excerpt from *The Circle*, a review of Native American News and Arts "dedicated to presenting reports from a Native perspective to its readers, while granting an equal opportunity to community voices."

Writes Mark Anthony Rolo: "The anti-treaty rights crusade is a blatant, racist attack on Native American sovereignty...They may loudly insist that they are not racist. They may even co-opt the voices of a few disgruntled Indians who have their own agenda...But no matter how sophisticated their public relations strategy, they cannot hide this truth: An anti-treaty rights stand is a racist stand."

Mr. Rolo ends his review by calling Bud Grant, the former Minnesota Vikings coach and supporter of equal treatment under the law for all Americans, "the leader of a racist movement. Despite his heartfelt pity for the Indian condition, Bud Grant is a racist."

These are strong words, especially when they offer no evidence to support the accusation.

Another *The Circle* article accuses the Citizens Equal Rights Alliance (CERA) of being "the largest, most organized, and most influential anti-Indian group in the U.S.…CERA has joined forces with the Alliance for America (AFA), a group fronted by Newt Gingrich and Republican Senators Slade Gorton (Washington) and Larry Pressler (South Dakota)." The only truth in this statement, according to the Alliance's current president, Bruce Vincent, is that CERA is a member of AFA. The rest is fiction.

The Circle goes on: "CERA is rumored to have ties with neo-Nazi and white supremacist groups…" Just by using the word "rumored," the author frees himself from the burden of proving the accusation while at the same time spreading—by mere mention—the unfounded rumor. Using the same tactic, we could say that "____________ (choose your own strongly-disliked public figure or organization here) is rumored to __________ (sin or barbaric activity)," and let other publications repeat this rumored rumor until the world takes it as fact.

The Center for Conservation Biology at Rice University sponsors an Internet site promoting a handbook for sale at the Center for Democratic Renewal in Atlanta, Georgia, titled *When Hate Groups Come to Town: A Handbook of Effective Community Responses.* "The Center for World Indigenous Studies…" an excerpt from the handbook reads, "has documented links between anti-Indian groups and Christian Identity and neo-Nazi organizations such as the Idaho-based Aryan Nations." It quotes the report as stating that "individuals associated with the anti-Indian movement now *appear* to have occasional, if not frequent association with right-wing extremist groups." [Emphasis added.]

Notice how the same technique is used here. Those associated with the anti-Indian movement—whatever that movement is—*appear* to have an association with extremists. It's not necessary to prove anything since it *appears* to be so. That is enough, despite the disclaimer at the end of the excerpt that says, "Anti-Indian groups deny any trace of racism." Just by using the term "Anti-Indian" in the disclaimer, the writer still maintains that the groups are racist. It is similar to saying "The misogynists deny any trace of hating women."

In addition, to brand everyone involved in a given movement a racist and anti-Indian because some true racists may have infiltrated the group, is the same as calling all Indians blood-thirsty cannibals based on the past behavior of just a few tribes.

There is a parallel here with the "Communist" tag used a few decades ago to silence opponents. Even John Collier, the crusader for the American Indian, got a taste of it, as he described it in *From Every Zenith*: "The Indian Bureau…charged that the American Indian Defense Association, which had just then been formed on Robert Ely's initiative, was a Soviet tool, and that our efforts with and for the Indians were machinations of Russian Communism. This charge was repeated, with slight variations as time went on, whenever the Indian Bureau was confronted with its own misdoings. Past the midpoint of the twenties, the usual wording was that the Indian Defense Association and the Pueblos were subsidized by Soviet money."

Today, that tag—that handy epithet to silence opponents—is the word "racist."

Racism can be defined in more than one way. Here we can use the following definition: using someone's or a group's race to justify an action—like special fishing and hunting rights—to the advantage or disadvantage of that someone or group against all others who don't share the same race.

White Supremacists

Since there were wide accusations of white supremacists being involved in the boat-landing protests in Wisconsin, the people of Minnesota made an extra effort to avoid public confrontation when it came to dealing with treaty claims.

"A deliberate decision was made to proceed through the proper channels," Bud Grant wrote in early 1997. "Those who opposed the tribal claims recognized that they could become easy targets to be tarred with the brush of racism by those who believe that anyone opposing treaty claims is wrong."

Accusations of racism tend to splash whole groups. After the Supreme Court did not grant certiorari in an appeal of the Tenth Circuit Court's ruling on *Crow Tribe of Indians v. Repsis*, which involved the 1868 treaty of the Crow Indians covering Wyoming territory, Arlo Dawes, the Executive Director of the Crow Tribe, said, "We are certainly shocked that the U.S. Supreme Court didn't want to hear the case. Treaty rights of Indian Nations are now at the whims of white supremacists, the courts and Congress and the President." Mr. Dawes chose to group together white supremacists with the courts, Congress and the President. In other words, everyone who does not agree with giving Indians different treatment under the law, based on race, is a white supremacist.

The case had been filed by the Crow Tribe on behalf of Thomas Ten Bear, one of its members. Ten Bear had been cited in 1989 by the Wyoming Game and Fish for killing an elk without a license. The tribe claimed that the 1868 Treaty gave them hunting rights, but the Tenth Circuit Court of Appeals had called those rights "temporary and precarious." Ten Bear and the Crow Tribe hoped the U.S. Supreme Court would review the case and reverse the Tenth Circuit Court's decision, but it was not to be.

Indian Country Today, which refers to itself as "America's Largest Indian Newspaper," described the Crow Tribe's setback with this headline: "A treaty that was supposed to be good as long as the grass grew and the rivers flowed was called 'temporary and precarious' by a court of appeals, and the U.S. Supreme Court agreed." The headline was a calculated lie. The words "as long as the grass grows and the rivers flow" are nowhere in the 1868 Treaty, or in any other treaty signed by the United States government with any tribe. What other purpose could such a headline have other than to incite racial animosity?

Who Is Indian?

The firm AAG International Research has a sales pitch: "We specialize in Native American research and proving Native American ancestry, American Indian genealogy or American Indian heritage *for Bureau of Indian Affairs 'BIA' benefits such as Minority Status, Low Interest Business Loans & Educational Grants*." [Emphasis added.]

"Once your Native American ancestry is proven and your quantum blood is determined," their literature says, "your Native American ancestry enables you and possibly other American Indian descendants who are related to you to qualify for tribal membership and receive benefits…"

Aspiring applicants don't need to bother with this company's services, however. The Department of Interior's Bureau of Indian Affairs (BIA) can provide most of the information they need to achieve the same goal, free of charge. That is, paid for by taxpayers.

To begin with, most tribes have their own membership requirements. A "blood quantum" (amount of Indian blood) is not even necessary, as in the case of adoption, whose tradition goes back to the times of Mary Jemison, a white girl who became a Seneca after she was kidnapped in a raid in 1758, when her family was murdered and she was given to two Seneca sisters who adopted her.

The BIA explains who qualifies as an Indian:

"No single Federal or tribal criterion establishes a person's identity as an Indian," the Bureau says. "Government agencies use differing criteria to determine who is an Indian eligible to participate in their programs. Tribes also have varying eligibility criteria for membership. To determine what the criteria might be for agencies or Tribes, you must contact them directly."

This is the clearest example of the bizarre policies that govern the different treatment of citizens under the law on the basis of race. How can policies be applied uniformly, even among American Indians, when the decision to classify someone as an Indian or non-Indian is left to the bureaucrat of the moment?

To complicate matters even more, the Bureau of the Census counts "anyone an Indian who declares himself or herself to be an Indian," according to the BIA. The 1990 census figures show there were nearly 2 million American Indians and Alaska Natives in the United States, a 37.9% increase over the 1980 census, thanks to more people declaring themselves as Indian.

But after saying all this, the BIA still has a list of requirements for those who wish to qualify for Bureau services, no matter what commercial genealogists and individual tribes may claim. According to the BIA, the applicant must…

- be a member of a Tribe recognized by the Federal Government;
- have one-half or more of Indian blood of tribes that are indigenous to the United States;
- be of one-fourth or more Indian ancestry, for some purposes;
- live on or near an Indian reservation, except in the case of Aleuts, Eskimos and Indians of Alaska.

The Bureau recommends the following steps to trace one's Indian ancestry:

- Basic genealogical research, if you do "not already have specific family information and documents that identify tribal ties." The research should include names of ancestors, dates of births, marriages and deaths, places where they lived, their brothers and sisters, if any, and, most importantly, tribal affiliations. "Among family documents to check are Bibles, wills, and other such papers."

What if these same requirements were set up for other Americans? Descendants of Polish immigrants, say? To qualify for a student or home-equity loan, the "Polish" American would have to prove his tribal affiliation to a Polish band.

Ethnic Translator

Fill in the blanks with your own genetic background. (The following paragraph is from the Bureau of Indian Affairs' Internet site—with references to the BIA and Indian Americans replaced with different ethnic references. Experience the special "government-to-government relationship" between ***your*** people and the government of the United States.)

The *Bureau of Polish Affairs* maintains a directory of *Polish-American offices*. When you know to which *Polish group* you may be a member, contact the *BPA*, Branch of *Polish* Enrollment, 1849 C St. NW, Washington, D.C. 20240 to get the address and phone number of the *Polish* membership office. Contact the *Polish* group to see if they have records of your ancestors. The key in determining *Polish* ancestry is identification of a specific *Polish* affiliation. Becoming a member of a *Polish* group is determined by the enrollment criteria of the group from which *Polish* blood may be derived, and this varies with each *Polish* group. Generally, if linkage to an identified *Polish* member is far removed, one would not qualify for membership, but it is the *Polish* group, not the *BPA*, which makes that determination.

An Indian Tribe was once defined as "a body of people bound together by blood ties who were socially, politically, and religiously organized, who lived together in a defined territory and who spoke a common language or dialect." This is no longer the case. When reservations were established, different tribes were sometimes put together on one reservation, or one tribe would be spread out over several reservations. As a result, tribes today cannot be as tightly defined as in the past.

This has led to a system of "federally recognized" tribes. There are now 556 of them in the United States. They have a "special, legal relationship with the U.S. government," so that federal recognition is viewed as a good thing. There have been more than 150 petitions to gain such recognition in the past two decades.

The BIA tells us that executive orders and administrative acts are being used to create reservations. At a time when the United States should be getting away from the anachronism of reservations, the goal of these acts and executive orders has been to expand federal control of state land, rather than give American Indians their full rights as citizens. "Indians can buy and hold title to land purchased with their own funds," the Bureau says. This is only as long as they don't meddle with reservation land. Nearly all tribal land is off limits to them, or anyone else. Tribal land is held "in trust" by the United States. "There is no general law that permits a tribe to sell its land," says the Bureau.

Those few who happen to own land individually on a reservation cannot sell it without the approval of the Secretary of the Interior. "If an Indian wants to extinguish the trust title to his land and hold title like any other citizen (with all the attendant responsibilities such as paying taxes), he can do so if the Secretary of the Interior or his authorized representative determines that he is able to manage his own affairs. This is a protection for the individual."

A more patronizing attitude than this can't be imagined. All that power vested on one passing bureaucrat, a Secretary controlling more than 55 million acres of "trust land" under the jurisdiction of the Bureau of Indian Affairs. Imagine if you had to ask permission from the President to sell your home, but he keeps on saying "No," because there exists a "special government-to-government" relationship between two government agencies that you have no control of.

Even when a reservation has a majority of non-Indians living on it, the state in which it is located has very limited powers over it. Indians and non-Indians on the reservation are subject to the local tribal government and the BIA. Non-Indians have no say in the makeup of the tribal government, however, even when they are forced to pay taxes to the tribe.

And do Indians pay taxes? Yes…and no. Almost every one of the "Frequently Asked Questions" on the BIA's Internet site are answered this way. Yes, Indians this-and-that…BUT….In the case of taxes, tribal members do not pay federal taxes "on income from trust lands held for them by the United States." They pay no state income taxes on income earned on a reservation. No state sales taxes on transactions made on an Indian reservation (many states have been fighting this in court). No local property taxes on reservation or trust land.

Do all laws apply to Indians and non-Indians alike? Yes… BUT, the Bureau says, "On Indian reservations…only Federal and tribal laws apply to members of the Tribe…." The Bureau does not mention what laws apply to the non-Indians who live on reservations (on average, forty-six percent of the population living on reservations and trust lands is non-Indian). That's because they live in a sort of legal limbo, subject to tribal and federal courts, not the state courts that their relatives may be subject to just a few miles away, off the reservation. One country, two sets of laws.

Some people may ask: "Why are those non-Indians living on reservations?" Their ancestors legally purchased or were allotted the land generations ago, when reservations were expected to become regular counties in just a few years.

The BIA goes on: "Any special rights that Indian tribes or members of those tribes have are generally based on treaties or other agreements between the United States and tribes." The 1837 Treaty was what brought the Mille Lacs Band of Chippewa to sue the State of Minnesota to reclaim treaty rights.

The folly of having two sets of laws based on race was illustrated by two, separate district court decisions in Minnesota. One of them took the definition of race a step further—away from blood quantum and toward tribal membership instead. These contradictory decisions produced different treatment under the law among Indians themselves:

	"European" Blood	Mille Lacs Ojibwe Blood
Mille Lacs Band Member	¾ th	¼ th
Red Lake Band Member	¾ th	¼ th

The chart shows the same blood quantum ratios. Yet, a member of one band can fish and hunt outside tribal land under the tribe's code; a member of the other cannot.

"Both are citizens of Minnesota and the United States," Bud Grant writes in "Why We Oppose Tribal Hunting and Fishing Claims" (a response to an editorial that appeared in the Minneapolis *Star Tribune*). But in one case, the district court had determined that tribal membership was the deciding factor. "Based on trends with other tribes," Grant continues, "the percentage of Mille Lacs Ojibwe ancestry required to be a Band member will further diminish in the future."

Who is Indian? It's getting harder and harder to say. But if you look back far enough, you too can be Indian. According to the book *The Native Americans: An Illustrated History*, during colonial times, many people ignored the ban on intermarriage between Indians and whites, and "informal mixture occurred…It has been said that if Indians were defined as Negroes are usually defined ('one drop of non-white blood means they are not white'), the number of 'Indians' in the United States would number into the millions."

Wouldn't it be interesting if half or two-thirds of the U.S. population contacted the Bureau of Indian Affairs to demand different treatment under the law based on their One Drop?

And so, Who is Indian?

It is not a question that should be answered with two sets of laws.

Bureau of Indian Affairs

The Bureau of Indian Affairs was established in 1824 as part of the War Department, an indication that contact with Indians at the time was considered, for the most part, a military affair.

In March of 1849, the Department of Interior was created by an act of Congress, and the Bureau was transferred there. The Interior Department is the conservation agent of U.S. public lands and natural resources. It has jurisdiction over some 500 million acres, with about ten percent of that being held in trust for Native American tribes through the Bureau of Indian Affairs.

One of the BIA's Guiding Principles, as expressed by its Public Affairs Office, is "Integrity, accountability and excellence are never compromised."

Yet, for years now, the Bureau has been described as the worst and most corrupt federal agency. In 1994, it had a budget of $1.8 billion that, according to a 1995 *St. Louis Post-Dispatch* article, trickled down to tribal members at ten cents on the dollar. The Bureau still has to account for billions of dollars in assets that went "missing" and that are the subject of a class-action lawsuit filed by Native Americans in 1996. Some people believe that part of the missing funds has been used by Native sovereignty nationalists (without the knowledge of most tribal members) to file land- and treaty-rights claims against the states in federal courts.

U.S. District Judge Royce C. Lamberth issued orders to the Interior and Treasury departments to turn over pertinent records to establish the veracity of the plaintiffs' accusations regarding the missing funds. After more than two years of waiting for the documents, Judge Lamberth cited Interior Secretary Bruce Babbitt, Treasury Secretary Robert Rubin, and Assistant Secretary of the Interior Kevin Gover for contempt of court and for showing "flagrant disregard" for his orders. "These officials," Lamberth's seventy-six-page opinion read, "are responsible for seeing that the laws of the United States are faithfully executed. In this case, the laws—the orders of this court—were either ignored or thwarted at every turn by these officials and their subordinates."

Another of the BIA's Guiding Principles: "Continuous improvement in the quality of service is vital to our success." Large corporations are not the only ones producing meaningless Guiding Principles and Vision Statements these days. Management fads have permeated every level of the federal bureaucracy. The BIA's Vision Statement is a living contradiction to what goes on inside the organization, especially if we are to judge it by recent reports.

Vision: "We provide high quality services in a timely professional manner. We have the organizational flexibility to meet the changing needs of our customers. Our employees are committed, knowledgeable and empowered. Our policies are clear, consistent and supported throughout the organization."

Judge Royce Lamberth clearly disagreed, and so did the more than 300,000 tribal members who filed the class-action lawsuit to find out what happened to the missing funds.

Ethnic Supremacists

Native sovereignty nationalists qualify under this category. They are as detached from the feelings of the Native American population as white supremacists are from most Americans' perception of race. The "racist" epithet has been used to good effect by self-serving Native sovereignty nationalists, and it has increasingly polarized Indians and non-Indians.

It turns out, however, that Native sovereignty nationalists have the same goals as members of a group that calls itself White Aryan Resistance (WAR). A "Guest Editorial" on WAR's Internet "Hate Page," describes a member's position on Native Canadians:

> I have heard right-wing leaders in Canada speak out against Native Self-Government. I hear right-wing people, all the time, whine and complain about Natives getting special rights. Lately, a new right-wing group has sprung up in my area who not only want no special rights for Natives, but also advocate the abolishing of Indian reserves and want Natives to integrate into Canadian society (or White society, as a whole!). From a White racial standpoint, this position is insane! I believe that Native Self-Government is a great idea. And, as far as their special privileges go, that does more to divide Whites and Natives than to unite us. And, after all, isn't Separatism what we're striving for?

On the Aryan Nation's Internet site, Roger Roots states that "The intent of the Fourteenth Amendment is repugnant to the original U.S. Constitution and the Organic Law of the land."

Finally, Alex Curtis, Editor of *The Nationalist Observer*, a "bimonthly magazine and daily e-zine published for activists in the struggle to secure the White Race's survival and advancement," has this to offer: "Racial Separation is an idea that seeks living space for members of races that desire the racial and cultural preservation of their people. The converse of racial separation is racial amalgamation, which leads to the death of pure races and is a form of genocide."

Racial, ethnic, cultural, and spiritual superiority is what many European colonists claimed upon first encountering the indigenous peoples of the Americas. The claim had no validity then and has no validity now, even when Native sovereignty nationalists use it.

The Advantages of Institutionalized Racism

Institutionalized racism is good, we're constantly told. It is the one practiced by the U.S. government and its agencies. It uses that fantastic tool of divisiveness that we call the census. The once-every-decade head count allows the government to dictate who is to receive taxpayers' money according to race.

But even this useful racial tool has been accused of being racist. The 1970 census was criticized by scholar Vine Deloria, Jr., for "probably" undercounting "Indians by as much as 10 to 15 per cent."

The Bureau of the Census says that classification of the population by race "reflects common usage, not an attempt to define biological stock." A handy disclaimer.

In fact, since 1960, race figures provided by the census are based on self-identification—not what the census taker sees with his or her own eyes. You can claim to be whatever you want. That "One Drop" could help you identify yourself with the ethnic background of your choice.

As a result, the number of Native Americans has increased steadily with each census—from 344,000 in 1950 to about 524,000 in 1960, 1,420,000 in 1980, and almost two million in 1990. This isn't because the Native American population is growing faster than the general population, but because more and more people are identifying themselves as Indians.

A case in point is Vincent A. Sebastian, Jr. If he didn't tell you he is Native American, writes Leslie Goffe in the February, 1999, issue of *Emerge*, "you wouldn't know. He looks African

American. In fact, for most of Sebastian's 38 years, he was poor and black, but nowadays he's Indian, too." Sebastian is quoted as saying: "I saw myself, back then, as just black, Afro-American… Today I consider myself a black, Afro-American Indian."

"Why the bizarre racial transformation?" asks Goffe. "Cultural pride and ancestral roots are among the reasons, but some see a one-word answer: money. To be a Pequot [Indian] is to be part owner of a billion-dollar casino business that guarantees a job, free health care, education, and a housing subsidy—on or off the reservation."

In *The New Indians*, Stan Steiner writes, "The more questions asked about race, and the more freely Indians answered them, the larger the population. When in 1930 and 1940 no such questions were asked, the [American Indian] population accordingly declined."

Steiner blames the "methods and attitudes" of the census takers for the lower, earlier counts—a polite way to claim that census takers were racists. "Nowhere was this more obvious than in the counts of city Indians," he adds, "who were an increasingly large proportion of the total Indian population."

Why the obsession with classifying citizens by race? Why is race part of the census at all, if not to manipulate people and divide them and categorize them and diminish them?

The answer, for those who don't have casinos, is also money. A great deal of it is allocated by the federal government to favored groups. The larger the group, the more money it gets. This has led Native sovereignty nationalists to claim that census figures on Indians are too low. The claim will surely be repeated with the 2000 census, now that the U.S. Supreme Court has ruled out "statistical sampling" methods to count minorities. Sampling would have extrapolated a real head count into an idealized figure that fit the government's idea of diversity.

Native sovereignty nationalists have given their own population estimates, which reach totals of up to three times the Bureau of the Census' figures. The 2000 census is expected to show drastic changes in the number of Native Americans and other minorities. Until those numbers come in, however, these are the 1990 figures (revised in 1991).

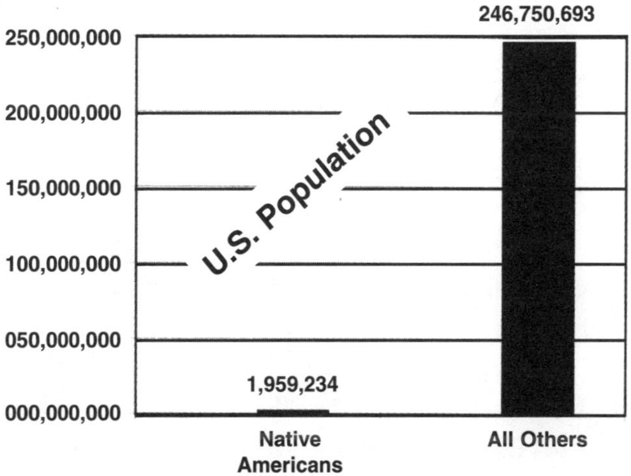

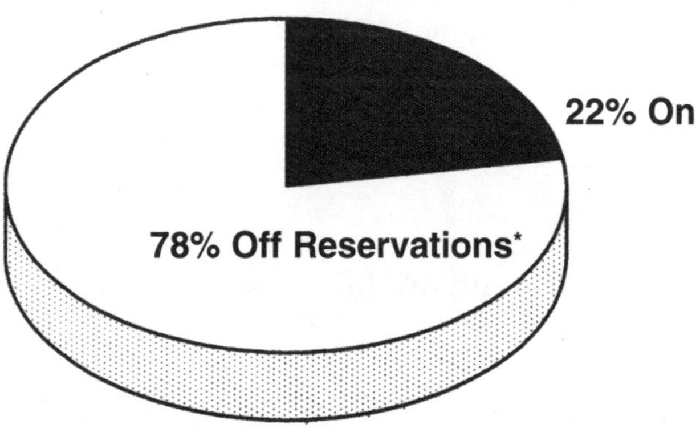

Where Native Americans Live

* In all graphs, "Reservations" includes federally identified areas and trust lands.

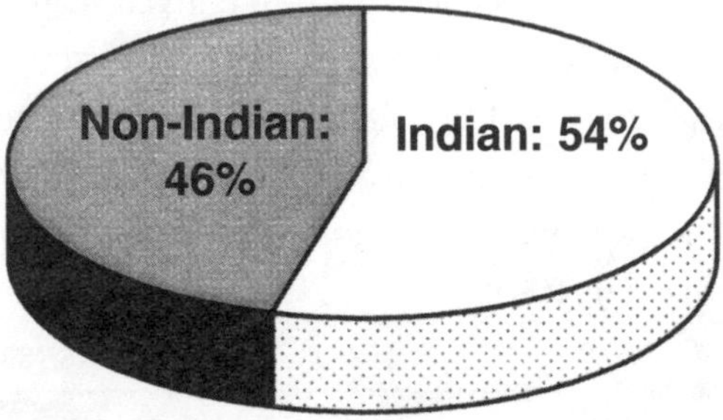

Makeup of Population on Reservations

It is considered extremely offensive and racist today to use census figures the "wrong" way. That is, to show that court decisions have blatantly given different treatment under the law to a very small number of citizens based on race.

In *United States v. Washington*, Federal Judge George Boldt, in what became known as the "Boldt Decision," ruled that Indians were entitled to "a fair share" (later defined as fifty percent) of Puget Sound's salmon harvest in Washington State. Using the racial figures offered by the U.S. Bureau of the Census (1991 release), the following graphs come up:

Makeup of Population in Washington State

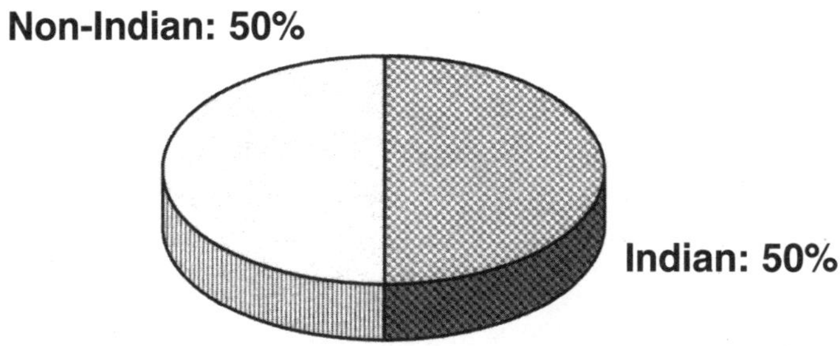

Puget Sound's Court-Ordered Salmon Harvest Allocation

The absurdity of producing a racial head count becomes even more apparent with the "Hispanic" category. Since there is no such thing as a Hispanic race, the U.S. Bureau of the Census uses the Spanish language to define such a group. If you or your ancestors came from a Spanish-speaking culture, then you are Hispanic, regardless of race. A black woman from the Dominican Republic is as "Hispanic" as the man in Argentina whose parents immigrated from Italy or a member of the very white Spanish Royal family, whose queen came from Greece.

The census, when it places so much importance on race, turns into little more than a tool to manage people like cattle: "More fodder for the Hispanic cows. They're not producing enough milk!"

Special Relationship With Nature

In *This Country Was Ours: A Documentary History of The American Indian*, Virgil Vogel makes the disingenuous statement that "Indian use of resources was different from ours." Of course. That would be the case with any two groups of people at different stages of technological and industrial development.

But in Vogel's view, everything the non-Indian does is analogous to the rape of nature. For the Indian, he writes, "the rivers and lakes were canoe routes and sources of food. We have turned them into foul sewers. The Plains were a hunting ground. There, we overcultivated and turned the region into a dustbowl scarred by wind and rain. Recognizing no value in forests except as lumber, we cut them down and unleashed floods in our river valleys."

Vogel's view of American Indians conforms to that of the noble savage—the belief that race or culture dictates appreciation and harmony with nature: Only if the blood quantum is right, can one be in tune with nature.

To deal with the noble savage image, Elliot West offers a dose of reality in *The Contested Plains: Indians, Goldseekers and the Rush to Colorado*. In a mere fifty years, he writes, Indians cut down sixty miles of Big Timbers that stretched from Kansas on the Arkansas River to the Purgatoire River in Colorado. This happened before the Gold Rush of 1858, when most of the non-Indians arrived. West's conclusion is that Colorado's Plains Indians "were not muscled onto reservations because soldiers defeated and sometimes butchered them. They ended up there because they lost command of the resources they needed to live as they wished."

The Native sovereignty nationalists' creed of a special relationship with nature, their better-than-thou attitude, is openly expressed every time the media gives them an opportunity. When the Mole Lake Chippewa were fighting Exxon's plans to mine zinc-copper sulfide near the Mole Lake Reservation in Northern Wisconsin, it was no exception. Whatever environmental merit their opposition to the mine had, they weakened it with comments like, "We will lose everything here if the mine happens, everything that Mother Earth has given us." Mother Earth doesn't "give" anything to any specially designated group. It simply sits there.

Instead of limiting the arguments to facts—like what effect the 2,000 gallons of wastewater that the mine would pump per minute would have on local water levels—the tribe's public relations approach was to hold an international conference on "environmental genocide" and argue that wild rice, from the beds that would be affected by the mine, was a "sacred food."

Native Americans can do no wrong to the environment or wildlife, we're often told. Even the environmental organization Greenpeace decides not to get involved when a tribe is on what Greenpeace would otherwise consider the wrong side of ecologically-correct behavior. When members of the Makah, an Indian tribe 125 miles west of Seattle, decided to return to their roots by hunting whales, the *Washington Post* reported that Greenpeace had chosen to "sit this one out in part because [of its] strong respect for the sanctity of Native American rights and traditions."

Never mind that there was a U.S. ban on whaling. The tribe got an exemption from the International Whaling Commission, and the Clinton Administration applauded the exemption by giving the tribe a $310,000 grant to prepare for the hunt.

The tribe then "hired a Washington public relations firm to help defend their views," the Post added. All this when the Makah no longer depend on whale oil or meat for survival. "This is our heritage," a whaling crew member said. "We want it back." It didn't matter that the hunt wouldn't even be traditional since more than just harpoons would be used. The crew planned to take a .50-caliber armor-piercing assault rifle to "help make any kill faster."

And it did. The Makah killed their first gray whale—a "30-foot juvenile whale"—in seventy-five years on 17 May 1999.

How many small groups of Americans can get $310,000 of taxpayers' money to return to "the essence of who we are as a people"? What if a group of Basque descendants in Nevada or

Idaho decided to go whale hunting? After all, Basques are believed to have hunted whales before anyone else. Quite a few Nevadans may suddenly want to return to the essence of who they are as a people. They may want to get a government grant, too.

But they won't qualify. They're not Makah. They don't have a special relationship with whales, or nature. No one else in America can hunt gray whales.

Huge Debt

Much of the current literature dealing with the fate of Native Americans after Columbus tries to make the reader feel responsible for what happened hundreds of years ago. New Age historians insist on extrapolating "white" behavior of another era to the present, using it as a tool to justify massive moral reparation that solves nothing but leads to further racial resentment.

Some accounts depict whites as the invading masses of ego and greed, with Indians as their clueless victims. A few historians have gone so far as to produce laundry lists of technological and social developments that the white race owes to other races. These lists are awfully close to those prepared by white supremacists to claim the exact opposite.

According to New Age historians, Europeans borrowed everything from everywhere. The wheel, the alphabet, gunpowder, the compass, numerals, domesticated plants and animals, cotton weaving, the printing press, rubber, paper, manner of dress, snowshoes, tobacco, hammocks, kayaks and canoes, pecans, peanuts, chocolate, chewing gum, avocados, popcorn, beans, tomatoes, potatoes—all owed to indigenous peoples.

"Frontier hospitality, and neighborly cooperation, such as barn-raising, were copies of Indian manners," we are told by historian Virgil Vogel. And Felix Cohen writes in *The American Scholar* that "Universal suffrage for women as for men, the pattern of states within a state that we call federalism, the habit of treating chiefs as servants of the people instead of their masters, the insistence that the community must respect the diversity of men and the diversity of their dreams—all these things were part of the American way of life before Columbus landed." We owe everything to native peoples, it seems. They "taught us progressive, non-authoritarian ways of rearing and teaching children," adds Vogel. They shaped our understanding of archeology, anthropology, linguistics, sociology, law, education, and political theory.

But so did the French, the Japanese, the Chinese, the Russians, the Pigmies, and countless others. To say that any one group owes anything to another ignores the nature of human communication. People get exposed to new ideas and then adapt them. Civilizations don't "borrow" the wheel and alphabet. People simply start using and adapting developments from the moment of exposure. And exposure to new ideas works in more than two ways. Knowledge travels in all directions and arrives from many. If news about the use of a wheel does not arrive from one group at one time, it will certainly come from another at a later time.

"Debts" lists were produced in response to the white historians' having "ignored" the indigenous peoples in their writings. And that's exactly the problem with virtually every book on Native American history since the early 1960s: they are a response to perceived indignities, not reports on actual history. A good part of the historical framework of the Native American experience rests on oral history. Most serious historians prefer to deal with physical evidence, not words from people who are alive now but were not then, when the events took place. This may be why they have been reluctant to write about American Indian history.

Racial History

Gripes about narrow-minded historians of the past who dismissed Indian contributions have produced the modern-day activist historian. This new version of scholar is as narrow minded as the old one is accused of being.

In his 1931 address to the American Historical Association, which was titled "Everyman His Own Historian," Carl Becker made the point that historians end up writing to please the masses, the book-reading public, whom he called Mr. Everyman. "Mr. Everyman is stronger than we are," Becker said, "and sooner or later we must adapt our knowledge to his necessities." This is used by modern-day historians to deem older history books as biased and written only to please white men.

Teaching history today is not so much a review of facts and evidence but an exercise in moral judgment and a demand for "justification." Americans in general are accused of not showing an interest in learning how the settlement of the New World was justified by Europeans. But historical events have no need to be justified. History simply *happens*.

When William Bradford wrote in the seventeenth century that he considered New England to be peopled by "only savage and brutish men," he was writing history from the European point of view. Instead of calling Bradford a biased racist, as some people do today, it would do better to study the context in which he made that observation. When old history books use phrases like "Indian menace" and "obstacle to settlement," they are merely reporting what was, in the context of those times, a fact: Indians were indeed an obstacle to white settlement. Whether white settlement was right or wrong is another matter. But the books are merely calling things by their name, and present-day, sensitivity-trained scholars get irate at these facts, for no reason at all.

It is a fact that Europeans of the 1600s believed Indians were savage and brutish men. They said so in their observations. Are we to erase that commentary from the historical record—replace it, even, with undocumented descriptions of fantastic indigenous kingdoms—just because we don't approve of how people expressed themselves a few hundred years ago?

We don't have to go that far back in history to show that it is a mistake to pressure the living to feel responsible for the beliefs of those long dead. Contemporary Germans are very sensitive about being described in terms of Germans of fifty years ago, and with good reason. A large number of them had not even been born then. They can be taught in schools about what took place during World War II. But there is a very fine line between teaching history and placing blame with the goal of producing collective feelings of guilt. Activist historians do their best to cross that line, to go far beyond it, without realizing the very real risk of producing a backlash, a moment when students will say, "So *what* if that happened!"

The drive to make certain groups feel responsible for the deeds of their ancestors is relentless. Publications such as *The Drum*, put out by the Rites of Passage Institute in Cleveland, Ohio, do their best to rub salt in what should be—for the social stability of America—long-healed wounds. In a piece titled "Democracy Was Not What They Had on Their Minds," assistant editor Marquita Hill reminds us that the authors of the U.S. Constitution were "wealthy white men of property" who established a system of politics that would ensure that "only their kind would sit in the White House."

The first part of her statement is a historical fact. The authors of the Constitution were indeed white men of property. The second is mere speculation since Hill offers no evidence to back her claim.

But let's say her assumption is correct and that the framers of the Constitution deliberately planned to exclude everyone other than "their kind" from political power, forever. If that was indeed the case, do we need to be reminded of it again and again? Are American citizens living today responsible for it? No. So what is the point of keeping the racial behavior of dead ancestors alive by means of constant reminders?

To put this in perspective, imagine that a foreigner who is a first-time visitor to America and recently arrived is taken to dinner at your home by a mutual friend. During the course of the evening, the foreigner has nothing good to say about the United States. "This country is awful—the crime, the racism, the corruption, the deviancy..." It is safe to say that you would soon feel offended by his comments. Who is *he* to say these things? If it were an American speaking that way, you might be annoyed by his comments but feel he's entitled to them. But this man? This recently arrived foreigner? Why doesn't he shut up? What is his point with all the criticism? What can he do about it? Nothing, unless he is planning to stay in America, become a citizen, and work to change things for the better. And if he dislikes America so much, why would he even want to stay? So shut up!

Much the same happens with race. There is absolutely no point in criticizing past behavior by one race toward another when the critics did not live in those times. People who insist, do so only to create divisiveness among the races in the present, which is the only moment in history that really matters to us. If there was racial strife then, the best way to avoid replicating it now is to stop referring to it, to stop pointing fingers.

Unfortunately, fingers are pointing everywhere, especially from the pages of school textbooks. At one point in the last couple of decades, Native sovereignty nationalists were able to force the educational system to teach their idea of American history.

Native American scholar Vine Deloria, Jr., complained in the '70s that children were being taught that "it was inevitable that Indians would be subjugated and become American citizens." That, in his view, had to change because Indian political allegiance was not American. Indians had never been subjugated. They still, in the 1970s, saw the United States as a foreign power. Children had to be taught this, Deloria said, and not the "sanitized version" that school books contained at the time.

As a child, John Collier had been taught the sanitized version. When he described his first "Pueblo Indian experience," he mentioned that, until that day, he had been still "possessed with the prevailing anthropological view [taught in schools then and before]...that all primitive and ancient cultures were doomed to be swallowed up by the white world."

Few of today's activist historians seem to realize that it is not "the white world" that is swallowing up cultures but technology—the same technology that is being used to constantly remind the masses that their ancestors were racist and that something must be done about it. The Greenwood Publishing Group, Inc., has an extensive Internet site listing textbooks that are meant to correct past wrongs. Some titles, like *How to Teach About American Indians*, are offered to "overcome the repetitious, inaccurate, and stereotypical curricula about American Indians found in many schools." A review of this textbook in *MultiCultural Review* assures school administrators that it will "inform students about the American Indian in a truthful manner, while maintaining the dignity of...Native American students who may be in a class, much as sensitivity workshops do."

The following event will probably never be heard of again in a schoolroom: In 1680, the Pueblo Indians slaughtered 500 Spaniards, many of them Catholic priests whose bodies ended up piled high on church altars. Another 2,000 Spaniards had to run for their lives from what is now New Mexico to El Paso, Texas. "Everything of Spanish manufacture or ownership—not only churches, houses, furniture, and art, but even swine and sheep—was destroyed. The god of the Spaniards was declared dead," writes Peter Farb in *Man's Rise to Civilization*.

In 1990, Wisconsin bands won the introduction of a mandatory public school curriculum fitting their views.

New Age Segregation

Special treatment based on race, like affirmative action, practically ensures that beneficiaries will never be accepted as equal under the law. They will only be resented by a large number of non-beneficiaries, and this will further divide the races.

Since the federal government denies reservation Indians the same rights that other American citizens have, the existence of reservations has often been compared to South Africa's old system of apartheid. The term "Apartheid" was coined long after the system itself had taken root in that country. Segregation based on race began with the arrival of Jan van Riebeeck and about 90 others who, in 1652, established a provisioning post for the Dutch East India Company on the Cape of Good Hope. The British continued the practice of segregating the races when they took control of the territory, establishing the first so-called black homeland.

The word Apartheid won currency in the elections of 1948, when the Nationalists took power. From that moment on, the policy of racial separation permeated every level of social relations in South Africa. Independent homelands (i.e., reservations) were established for blacks. Laws followed the same pattern.

In June of 1991, major changes were implemented to end the practice of apartheid in South Africa. The country still has a long way to go, but at least its government and most of its citizens are working in the right direction.

"Until recently," Les de Villiers and two co-authors write, "it has been fashionable in South Africa to argue about who laid claim to which portion of the country. This debate has subsided somewhat as the realization set in that it is as unrealistic to try and unscramble an egg as it is to divide all the different factions into neat separate areas according to historic rights and claims...."

In contrast, the United States' Federal Indian Policy is doing exactly the opposite—giving one group of citizens different treatment under the law—when we should know better. The fact that a Federal Indian Policy even exists today should give all Americans a cause for concern. How loud would the public protests be if a Federal Chinese-American policy were implemented? Or a German-American policy? Or if a Bureau of Chicano Affairs were established, and a Bureau of Oppressed Texans, for those few who insist that Texas is still a republic?

When one group is given special status under the law, then nothing can stop the creation of thousands of groups that will clamor for special attention. There lies the wisdom of the Fourteenth Amendment: it is infinitely simpler to strive for equal treatment for all than to define who has been oppressed, or who gets what and how much and when as a reward for past "wrongs."

Face Value

Federal Indian Policy has been so divisive, in fact, that any debate of recognizing Native Americans as part of the American landscape turns into controversy.

When the Department of the Treasury and the United States Mint was in the process of selecting a design for a new one-dollar coin in 1998, there was a big push by various interest groups to make the coin carry an Indian theme. The image of Sacajawea, the sixteen-year-old girl who joined the expedition of Lewis and Clark in 1804, was one of the options. Those who opposed using Sacajawea argued that few Americans would relate to or recognize the new coin. In their view, it was better to use the image of the Statue of Liberty.

Those in support of the American Indian theme showed how the belief of racial superiority dominates their ideas, even if it is at an unconscious level. Showing Sacajawea with her baby, the president of the National Congress of American Indians (NCAI) said, would be "consistent with the maternal qualities and compassion of American Indian women." But don't all mothers, regardless of race, have maternal qualities and compassion for their children?

About another Sacajawea design (one without her baby), NCAI's president said, "It reflects the pride and the courage and the dignity of the American Indian woman."

Opponents claimed that polls showed Americans favored the Statue of Liberty. But the United States Mint decided to hear directly from the masses by setting up an Internet site showing all seven final design options (three obverse, four reverse), Indian and non-Indian, allowing visitors to comment. "During the first days in which the potential designs were displayed online along with a request for comments," wrote Philip N. Diehl, the United States Mint Director, "the Mint received over 90,000 e-mailed responses. I am confident that the new coin will be an even better designed, better accepted, and a more usable product because of this [Internet polling] experience."

But any kind of poll or vote was meaningless since the final design was at the discretion of the Secretary of the Treasury.

A later report announced that Sacajawea had won.

Repatriation

Native Americans can write a letter to any museum and demand that their cultural heritage be returned to them at once. Thomas Killion, the director of the Repatriation Program at the Smithsonian, expresses his institution's spirit of cooperation: "We have worked with tribes across the country to return...culturally sensitive items affected by the repatriation legislation."

This legislation is the Native American Graves Protection and Repatriation Act (NAGPRA), passed by Congress in 1990. It provides that remains shown to have lineal descent, and artifacts with cultural affiliation to a native group must be returned to that group.

"Since repatriation began at Natural History," Killion writes, "we have returned more than 1,000 such objects as well as the skeletal remains of almost 5,000 Native Americans....The Smithsonian has a strong and long-standing policy on repatriation, and we have returned more objects and remains under the law than any other organization in the United States."

Non-Indian American citizens have not been favored with such race-based legislation. An American descendant of French immigrants cannot demand, under the law, that the French Legation Museum in Austin, Texas, for example, return items in the collection to her just because her ancestors were French.

Though NAGPRA has no jurisdiction overseas, the Lakota Sioux reached out to Scotland in 1998 to demand cultural heritage repatriation. When Native American John Earl was on vacation in Glasgow, he ran into an exhibit of a "Ghost Dance" shirt that had been reportedly worn by a Sioux killed in the massacre of Wounded Knee. A member of Buffalo Bill Cody's Wild West Show had taken the shirt to Scotland in 1892.

"When I first saw it, my heart stopped," Earl said. "It is of a value that is very difficult to communicate to someone who is not a Native American. It should not be in Glasgow."

So the legal wheels were set in motion to bring the shirt back, until the Glasgow City Council agreed to the demand.

Despite such favorable, racially-based legislation as NAGPRA, Native sovereignty nationalists still see every act that does not favor Indians as a form of genocide. When the United States Seventh Circuit Court of Appeals ruled on the Menominee Treaty Rights case in November of 1998, the Chairman of the Menominee Nation had this to say: "We should not be surprised as an Indigenous Nation that this case is another imperialistic fascist act of the dominant society attacking the minority and principles of National and International Law....Imperialists and fascists, I am sure are gloating over this victory which extends to all future cases....Today, I call on the United States Supreme Court of America to hear our case and correct the wrongs of the District and Seventh Circuit Court of Appeals. As Americans, we need not send the...same message that Hitler sent to his people in Germany. Lets [sic] not allow our Judicial system to sit at the gates of Dachau and Auschwitz in the name of equal justice for all."

The Hitler comparison pops up often in the arguments of Native sovereignty nationalists. And the genocide goes on, according to *When Hate Groups Come to Town*, the handbook sponsored by Rice University's Center for Conservation Biology: "For the most part," the handbook says, "Native Americans were subdued by a combination of disease, alcohol, food rationing, the cooperation of Indian collaborators, and the theft of children for boarding schools—*a situation not radically unlike today*." [Emphasis added.]

Elizabeth Gray, co-publisher of the *Oklahoma Indian Times*, goes even further: "German Nazis studied how America treated the Indian people and used those examples in their treatment of The Jews....You think I'm being dramatic," she writes, "then you should also call 'Schindler's List' an over-dramatized account of the Jewish Holocaust."

Shaky Status

How "native" are Native Americans? Don't ask. The answer could mean that the excuse used to treat indigenous groups differently under the law has no basis.

In 1996, the remains of a Caucasian man were found near Kennewick, Washington State. At first, the bones were believed to belong to a white settler of 100 years ago. But the University of California, using radiocarbon dating, found them to be from 9,300 to 9,600 years old.

The skeleton was given the name "Kennewick Man" and became the center of a controversy pitting scientists against Native sovereignty nationalists over who had rights to it.

Kennewick Man is clearly the ancestor of non-Indians, whose remains are "impossible to match among any of the Western American Indian tribes," as one Washington State University anthropologist put it.

If the most respected theory that American Indian ancestors crossed a land bridge from Asia to America is right, then Kennewick Man could be evidence that there were other races on the continent before they arrived. But some Native sovereignty nationalists oppose the land bridge theory. Their claim is that their ancestors were here first, no matter what.

Consequently, the threat of Kennewick Man—the scientific study that could jeopardize their basis for sovereign and treaty rights—must be reburied at once, before scientists have a chance to find out more. The Confederated Tribes of the Umatilla Indian Reservation claimed that the skeleton belonged to their ancestors since it was found on their traditional land, and must be returned to them under the Native American Graves Protection and Repatriation Act, the same piece of race-based legislation that has the Smithsonian Institution returning art objects and skeletal remains to American Indian tribes.

The Act says that the human remains found on federal or tribal land must be shown to have lineal descent *before* they can be claimed. How can lineal descent be determined with a skeleton believed to be over 9,000 years old if not with computer measurements and DNA studies?

The U.S. Army Corps of Engineers administers the land where Kennewick Man was found. Corps officials were considering returning the remains to the tribe when lawsuits were filed to stop them. One suit was brought by eight well-known scientists. Another by followers of the Asatru religion, who believe Kennewick Man may be one of their Scandinavian or Germanic ancestors.

Alan Schneider, the attorney for the scientists, said that Native Americans assume that "anyone who died in this country prior to 1492 [the year of Columbus' arrival] is native American within the meaning of the statute, and of course that's not necessarily true."

When the popular television program *60 Minutes* picked up the story, Elizabeth Gray, the co-publisher of the *Oklahoma Indian Times*, didn't like Leslie Stahl's report at all. "This report was laced with personal biase [sic] opinion," she wrote, "and was not sought to give news to the public but to express the reporter's personal, prejudice [sic] viewpoints on the matter while swaying the story with leading comments."

Gray strongly objected to the report's contention that the reason American Indians did not want Kennewick Man studied might be based more on fears of losing their different treatment under the law than on religious beliefs. "Let me enlighten [Stahl] and the producers on a bit of facts about Native Americans," Gray added. "According to a recent presidential report from the White House, Native Americans are the worst treated minority race in the United States. They have the highest poverty rate, highest alcoholism, highest death rate, etc..." Gray doesn't explain how this White House report is relevant to the scientific study of skeletal remains. Again, the implication is that all non-Indians should feel guilty about the condition of Native Americans and thus let the tribes have their way (i.e., bury Kennewick Man right away) because they deserve it.

"As a news provider to the American public," Gray continues, "you should be ashamed for slandering a race of people who have been slandered to death....America's first and most abused citizens."

Kennewick Man is only the most publicized case. There are many other discoveries which are far more important to the theory that the continent was long ago populated by a diverse pool of races. The oldest human remains known in North America are skull fragments up to 11,500 years old. They are said to belong to Spirit Cave Man, and they were found in 1940, though it wasn't until 1994 that radiocarbon dating was performed on them.

Spirit Cave Man's skull does not match contemporary Native Americans' skull shapes, either. Between the races, skull shape is very distinctive and hereditary. It goes almost unaffected by environmental factors in the evolutionary scheme of a few tens of thousands of years. Researchers, taking up to ninety measurements per skull, can determine whose ancestor Spirit Cave Man is. Two other skulls found in Minnesota had measurements closer to Europeans or Indonesians than Native Americans.

Additional evidence has come to us in the form of spear points. Some very unusual ones have been found a few miles south of Richmond, Virginia. Preliminary dating estimated them to be some 15,000 years old. They don't look like anything else found on the continent, but a lot like stone tools found in Spain dating from 16,500 to 24,000 years old.

So it seems that America, long before Columbus, had racial diversity. At some point, the ancestors of today's Native Americans overwhelmed all the other races, either through war or intermarriage, and that is why they were dominant when Columbus arrived.

The Native American Graves Protection and Repatriation Act, long requested by Native sovereignty nationalists, backfired on the tribes: Once Native sovereignty nationalists started demanding repatriation of anything found by anthropologists, the scientific community rushed to test and date (with radiocarbon) all skeletons and artifacts that had been found to date before they were lost to the tribes. The results of those tests are coming back to haunt the sovereignty nationalists.

As International Research's Internet genealogy site says, "Native American descendants are entitled to both Tribal and Bureau of Indian Affairs (BIA) benefits...your Native American or American Indian lineage must be proven to obtain these benefits." What happens when lineage and ancestry are found to mean nothing? This is where the fear lies, the fear of finding out that the whole edifice of First-Americanness can collapse thanks to increasingly sophisticated archeological and anthropological research. So-called First Americans are hearing it more and more: their ancestors may very well not be the first inhabitants of the land but simply a passing, dominant, occupying force—as temporary and contemporary in the vast history of the planet as the dominant cultures of the present will be someday.

Helping the Needy

Many federal programs are driven almost solely by racial considerations—ones that, for obvious reasons, very few people question. When a Washington, D.C., government official sees the need to resign over his use of the word *niggardly*, simply because it is too close to the "N" word, what can anyone expect from pointing out the overt racism of government policy? (*Niggardly* was defined as *stingy, parsimonious* by all dictionaries when the official used the word in early 1999.)

Most citizens accept the idea that the federal government should help the needy, that funding from the Department of Housing and Urban Development (HUD) should go to those who, for one reason or another, cannot afford basic housing needs.

But that's not the case with the 1996 Native American Housing Assistance and Self-determination Act (NAHASDA), which is funded by HUD. The Act was approved to promote affordable housing opportunities for American Indians and consolidate all Indian housing development programs under one better organized agency.

The Potawatomi tribe was one of the first to take advantage of the Act. Enrolled members could, as a result, purchase a home with as little as one percent of their own money. This is very useful for those who cannot afford anything else. But the $5 million Potawatomi initiative was reported by *Business Wire* as being "targeted to all Citizen Potawatomi tribal members living in Oklahoma, *regardless of income*." [Emphasis added.] In other words, race is the only consideration in giving HUD money—taxpayers' money—away.

The First Americans Mortgage Corporation (FAMC) assisted in the development of the program with the Housing Authority, a Potawatomi Nation's joint news release stated. The program was the third that FAMC had secured under similar arrangements.

More were to come—one involving the Chickasaw Nation ($10 million), and one the Choctaw Nation ($10 million).

"FAMC is excited about this unique opportunity to make affordable housing loans to members of the Potawatomi Nation," said Dustan R. Shepherd, founder and president of FAMC. "Being a Native American owned company, FAMC is extremely pleased to be working with one of just seven Native American owned banks in the United States," he added. "As the only federally-chartered bank that is 100% Native American owned and managed, First National will be a role model for serving Indian Country's housing needs."

Let's run this statement through our racial translator:

"Being a *White* owned company, *WAMC* is extremely pleased to be working with one of just seven *White* owned banks in the United States....As the only federally-chartered bank that is 100% *White* owned and managed, *White* National will be a role model for serving the *White Man* Country's housing needs."

What would the fate of Dustan R. Shepherd be, as president of *any* organization, if he said such a thing as this racially-translated statement?

FAMC is not the only player in the Native American home loan business. Fannie Mae and the U.S. Department of Agriculture's Rural Housing Services offer a guaranteed-loan program—with no down payment—for homes on Indian reservations.

Legal issues in lending are no longer the barriers they once were, reports the *Washington Post*. "Model documents and ordinances now establish the legal framework for lending *while respecting issues of importance to tribes, such as restricting ownership to tribal members*." [Emphasis added.] This is in reference to the fact that, on most reservations, individual Indians do not own the land they live on. The U.S. government holds it permanently in trust. Taxpayers, through HUD and the Department of Agriculture, are actually funding home-ownership programs that *restrict* ownership.

The Bureau of Indian Affairs also has a bureaucratic say on whether a Native American qualifies for a mortgage or not, even if that individual has already been approved by Fannie Mae. The excuse is that the BIA doesn't want Native Americans to be taken advantage of by bankers. As a result, the loan applicant must file an additional application with the BIA, in which the Bureau asks about the percentage of Indian blood of the applicant, work habits, mental health, and use of alcohol, according to Jan Sieberts at the National Bank of Alaska.

The "Good Guys"

The "pro-Indian" movement, we are told by the Midwest Treaty Network, contains support groups who concern themselves with the following:

- Countering racism.
- Opposing cultural and religious bias against Indian people.
- Supporting Treaty Rights.
- Opposing "anti-Indian" groups.

These goals don't include equal treatment under the law because that's not what these groups are interested in, even when it is impossible to counter racism while demanding Treaty Rights (i.e., different treatment under the law based on race).

The Wait — Expectations

The Minneapolis *Star Tribune* mentioned the Mille Lacs Supreme Court hearing on the day it took place, 2 December 1998, and on the following day. Few other major newspapers bothered with it.

If supporters of the Fourteenth Amendment have failed at anything, it is in not being able to make their case one of national interest when it comes to Federal Indian Policy. Treaty lawsuits are still perceived as a local issue. Even online publications run by Native American news services did not report the Supreme Court hearing the day after it took place. Internet sites are relatively easy and inexpensive to update, and the hearing had the potential of affecting all Indian tribes of the United States. Yet, *News From Indian Country* and the *Oklahoma Indian Times* had no fresh news to offer that day. Even the *New York Times* and *Washington Post* and *Denver Post* had nothing to say about the case.

As the long wait for a decision went on, there seemed to be a consensus that the Supreme Court would reverse the lower court's ruling. The State of Minnesota, the counties and landowners would win the case, and so would the idea of equal treatment under the law for all citizens.

Everyone was aware that a total victory for the Fourteenth Amendment required a reversal based on the Equal Footing Doctrine argument. The Court's justices, however, had not asked a single question pertinent to that subject.

Why is it necessary to affirm the Fourteenth Amendment by using the Equal Footing Doctrine argument? Because it is the only way to stop the treaty-claims lawsuits that have been filed and will continue to be filed across the country. One tribe has even claimed rights from a treaty signed with the King of England, long before the United States became a country. The Mattaponi Indians of Virginia—aided by the Sierra Club—claim that a treaty signed in 1677 is still binding and that it prohibits white settlement within a three-mile area of any local Indian town. The treaty had not been enforced since the seventeenth century, but the tribe decided to resurrect it in 1998. Today, dozens of non-Indians live and own property in the three-mile "buffer zone."

"One of the least understood facts about Indian treaties," writes William C. Canby in *American Indian Law in a Nutshell*, "is that they may be abrogated unilaterally by Congress....Many people assume that any alterations in terms would have to be mutually negotiated by the federal government and the tribes. The law, however, is to the contrary." Canby is a former professor of law at Arizona State University and now a member of the Ninth U.S. Circuit Court of Appeals.

Judge R. A. Randall, of the Minnesota Court of Appeals, gives an example in his 1996 dissent in *Cohen v. Little Six, Inc.*: "The final word on treaties is best expressed by the United States Supreme Court in *Lone Wolf v. Hitchcock* [1903], when it states that when all is said and done, Congress has complete power over Indian tribal property and Congress can abrogate the provisions of an Indian treaty at any time."

There are several examples in which courts have recognized Congress' power to abrogate Indian treaties. Among them:

- *The Cherokee Tobacco* (1871): Termination of treaty right to tax exemption.
- *Brendale v. Confederated Tribes and Bands of the Yakima Indian Nation* (1989): Ending of treaty right to total control of all allotted land (Indian and non-Indian) on a reservation.
- *Montana v. United States* (1981): Same.
- *Oregon Department of Fish and Wildlife v. Klamath Indian Tribe* (1985): Termination of treaty right to hunt and fish on ceded land under the tribe's own conservation code.
- *South Dakota v. Bourland* (1994): Ending of treaty right to regulate non-Indian hunting and fishing on reservation land once it has been taken by the United States for public use.

The problem is that Congress rarely says, "Here, we are passing this law and such-and-such treaty is abrogated as a result." Most laws that affect treaties have been passed without any reference to any treaty. The courts are left with the burden of interpreting whether Congress meant abrogation or not.

This can be solved by passing a simple act abrogating all Indian treaties at once, finally making Native Americans full citizens of the United States, treated equally under the law. The Equal Footing Doctrine could be a vehicle for such an act.

Why Are We Here?

We are here—geographically—for the same reason we are here spiritually: it just happened. Those now living in the United States who are descendants of immigrants had no control over the process, and can only deal with it from the here and now.

Everyone is in agreement that, to get here, horrible things happened to people, to whole cultures and civilizations. But the process of invasion, conquest, and colonization was not all hatred and greed. Millions of immigrants participated in the populating of the Americas. To accuse them all of inflicting genocide on those who were already here is to disregard some basic principles of human nature.

In *Coyote Medicine*, Lewis Mehl-Madrona, M.D., describes his views on the benefits of integrating Native American healing practices with conventional medicine. He writes about an old medicine man who once told him that before a person can heal, "he or she must answer three simple questions."

- Who are you?
- Where did you come from?
- Why are you here?

These are wonderful questions because they cannot be answered with finality. In trying to answer them, we define ourselves as part of a whole that cannot be controlled by anyone.

Human activity and responsibility—in the overall view of things—have an insignificant role.

Like Going to The Moon

When in the summer of 1969 human civilization first landed on the moon (as far as we know), no one was thinking of the mass killing of potentially unknown organisms on the lunar surface. The assumption was that there was no life on the moon. But if some organism had been found on landing, it would have been almost irrelevant next to the excitement generated by that first contact.

It is mostly the power of human curiosity that drives exploration and discovery, not greed and a thirst for domination. In trying to answer Mehl-Madrona's three questions, new ones are formulated: What else is out there? How much don't we know? How far can we go? Can we reach land by sailing west?

The same joy of discovery that drives us to send space probes to Mars today is what pushed explorers in the "Old" world to make their way to the "New." It is an aspect of human nature that will not go away. To decry its consequences (i.e., the resulting here and now) is similar to saying that thinking is evil because some people are liable to have evil thoughts.

The excitement of discovery doesn't require going to the end of the world or to outer space. It can be found under our own feet. In late 1998, the *Washington Post* reported that archeologists were "excited about the discovery of eight underground silos near Fletcher's Boat House on the C&O Canal [in Washington, D.C.]." The silos were five feet deep and seven feet across, and around 2,000 years old, from a time when "American Indians were not known to have lived in villages or to have used storage pits." What the silos were used for, or why "American Indians kept building new ones, is a mystery—and another reason for the excitement about the discovery," the report said.

Much of this same excitement and feelings of wonder were also part of the human experience at the time Europeans began to hear about the Americas. Many reports from the lands newly discovered by Europeans whetted the appetites of those left behind. Settlers encouraged their friends and relatives to join them.

The Reverend Francis Higginson arrived in Salem in 1629. He found the air there to be extraordinarily clear and dry, and "of a most healing nature to all such as are of a cold, melancholy, phlegmatic, rheumatic temper of body."*

Higginson promoted the American continent to his friends in England as a "healthful" place. "My friends that knew me," he wrote, "can well tell how very sickly I have been...much troubled with a tormenting pain through an extraordinary weakness of my stomach...but since I came here on this voyage, I thank God I have had perfect health."

Letters home and official reports also included descriptions of what to Europeans was exotic Indian behavior. David de Vries described (in 1655) what is today known as a Native American sweat lodge: "When they wish to cleanse themselves of their foulness, they go in the autumn, when it begins to grow cold, and make...near a running brook, a small oven, large enough for three or four men to lie in...they take a parcel of stones, which they heat in a fire, and then put in the oven, and when they think that it is sufficiently hot [inside], they take the stones out...and go and lie [inside], men and women, boys and girls, and come out so perspiring, that every hair has a drop of sweat on it. In this state they plunge into the cold water, saying that it is healthy, but I let its healthfulness pass; they then become entirely clean, and are more attractive than before."

** Old English spelling throughout the book has been changed to modern English.*

Much earlier than this, Pedro de Castañeda described Pueblo Indian kitchens as they were encountered during a 1540 expedition: "They keep the separate houses where they prepare the food for eating and where they grind the meal, very clean. This is a separate room or closet, where they have a trough with three stones fixed in stiff clay. Three women go in here, each one having a stone, with which one of them breaks the corn, the next grinds it, and the third grinds it again. They take off their shoes, do up their hair, shake their clothes, and cover their heads before they enter the door. A man sits at the door playing on a fife while they grind, moving the stones to the music and singing together."

Let's say that a planet is discovered today that is believed to hold human life. The planet is reachable in six months' time thanks to new space-travel technology (it took Columbus thirty-six days to cross the Atlantic from the Canary Islands). There would be a global rush. Then, someday, you receive a letter from a friend who has been living on the "new" planet for a year. She tells you wonderful things about the place—endless rain forests with delicious tropical fruits, constantly pleasant weather, a sort of radiance to the atmosphere that energizes the body and mind, etc. Is she exaggerating? The "new humans" she has found there look very much like us, she says, although they have a few unusual practices.

A year later, you see an ad posted on cyberspace: "Passage to New Planet. Only $200. Affordable land for settlement." If you are the adventurous type (as most of those who came to the Americas were), you will go for the experience, the thrill of doing something few others have done before. You will be followed by millions, billions, even. There is enough nomadic blood in the human race to keep a constant flow of people moving to wherever there is transportation for all eternity.

Would you, or anyone else, be thinking about the consequences, especially if there is a growing perception that *our* planet is already spent and we better expand to new frontiers or perish?

The United States was founded on the urge to explore new frontiers, to try new systems of government, to investigate all that science hints at. Native sovereignty nationalists want to go back to the past. But we can't. Cultures will continue to evolve, to intermingle and affect each other, for better or worse. That's who we are, where we come from, and why we are *all* here.

The Better Known Arrival

"Columbus' actions launched an era of modern colonialism, rape, pillage, genocide, cultural destruction, slavery, economic and environmental devastation....To celebrate Columbus is...the same as having Jews celebrate Hitler and the [H]olocaust. Columbus is much more than a representation of evil; he is the very embodiment of that evil."

So writes Marc Becker at *The Hartford Web Publishing* Internet site, a company that generates "web pages that promote social progress" and is publisher of "the Communist Party of Connecticut, Communist Party USA..." Internet sites.

The movement to make Columbus the butt of all hatred gained strength at the beginning of the 1990s, as the 500th anniversary of his arrival in the Americas approached.

Columbus was known as an ambitious and ruthless man, but once he founded the first few colonies claimed for Spain, the situation was out of his hands. Even on Hispaniola, where he was Governor General, many colonists were only interested in finding gold and disobeyed his orders. On his third voyage, the Spanish Crown forced him to take convicts to further colonize the New

World. By 1500, he was out of favor and was replaced by an independent governor before being sent back to Spain—in chains. Efforts to restore his reputation with additional voyages were not very successful. Other explorers were playing the game by then.

In his letter dated 14 March 1493, Columbus described his first impressions of the indigenous people he encountered in the New World:

"These people are so amiable and friendly that even the King took a pride in calling me his brother...I did not find, as some of us had expected, any cannibals among them, but on the contrary, men of great deference and kindness."

This is a letter from the same man whom Columbus Day protesters describe with graffiti such as "Columbus = Genocide" and "Columbus = Red Holocaust."

The Italian explorer has become the handy whipping boy of the masses as the "starter of it all." He was not even the first European to come to the Americas. The fact that he is used as the target of collective anger shows how much in need of symbolism the whole us-versus-them movement is in order to keep itself going.

Columbus is cursed for having taken Indians back to Spain to show to Queen Isabella. The Indians were "dressed in full regalia and decorated with war paint" and "quickly [became] the curiosities of Spain," writes Peter Farb in *Man's Rise to Civilization.*

Today, no one curses the environmental activists who do the same. In late 1998, Juan Pablo Orrego, an eco-warrior with *Grupo Acción Por el Bío-Bío*, took Nicolasa Quiltramán, a Mapuche Indian from central Chile, on a publicity tour through Spain, Holland, Germany, and Sweden—an international spectacle staged to raise funds for green activism. Orrego was on his way to participate in a ceremony for the Right Livelihood Prize (a.k.a. the "Alternative Nobel"), which was given to the Grupo that year.

After Columbus, settlers from various parts of Europe rushed to the Americas. Among them were…

- France's Jacques Cartier, landing at Quebec on 7 September 1535;
- Spain's Hernando De Soto's expedition, establishing contact with Muskhogean and Cherokee tribes between 1539 and 1543;
- England's Sir Richard Grenville and Sir Ralph Lane, landing at Roanoke Island in the summer of 1585; and
- English settlers disembarking in May of 1607 at what later became Jamestown, Virginia.

Settlement

The number of people living in what is now the continental United States in 1492 is a subject of debate. Estimates go from one million to fifteen million.

Whatever the number, the founding of Jamestown in 1607 was the first step in the creation of a political and social system that would eventually affect all of them. Jamestown was the first permanent English settlement in the so-called New World. The Spanish and French monarchies also established permanent settlements, but they had different purposes. The Spanish colonial powers were more a tool for natural-resource exploitation than for expanding colonization. The French, too, were more interested in trading fur with the Indians than in establishing permanent settlements. Quebec was just a hub of easy access to the St. Lawrence River, which was used to reach the Great Lakes and the Ohio River Valley.

At first, Indians helped the Jamestown settlers by showing them what foods were available—plants and animals that

Europeans had never seen before—and how to get them.

"The pattern of white relations with the [Virginia] Indians,..." writes historian Virgil Vogel, "was, with few exceptions, characteristic of the relations that were to prevail everywhere for three centuries. In the stage of weakness, friendly relations were to be maintained in the interest of self-preservation." This is obvious. What else could the settlers do? There was an uneasy co-existence between the two groups from the beginning. The Powhatan Confederacy, as the tribes around Jamestown became known, could have easily destroyed Jamestown in its early days.

But no devastation came to the colonists, despite occasional skirmishes and the taking of prisoners by both sides. John Rolfe, a Jamestown tobacco grower, married Pocahontas, Chief Powhatan's daughter, in 1614. The marriage kept the peace for eight more years, despite Pocahontas' death in 1617, and her father's in 1618.

By then, the settlers were exploring farther inland. The urge to find out what else was out there, plus the search for additional resources, was the main thrust in the colonists' expansion. But there was also an element of racial competition involved. Both natives and newcomers, writes Paula Mitchell Marks in *In a Barren Land: American Indian Dispossession And Survival*, "possessed a sense of ethnic superiority." The Europeans, however, once they were strong enough, had the technology to allow them to dominate.

While the Indians gave the colonists the right to use the land for hunting, fishing and planting, the European mind was not at ease without the security provided by having title to the land. The idea of private property as a guarantor of liberty developed from the Magna Carta, to which the English had been exposed since 1215. Sharing property in the New World, even among themselves, was not an option.

"The colonists and the mother countries," writes historian Vine Deloria, Jr., "were faced with the problems of defining the rights of Europeans against Europeans in conflicting claims in the New World." In defining those European rights, the question of Indian title to the land had to be considered. "No settler wanted to settle or purchase lands which might have some aspect of Indian title remaining with them," adds Deloria. "Nor did the colonists want to suffer the accusation by the European nations that they had swindled the inhabitants of the New World."

The way to solve this problem, in many cases, was to define Indians as less human than the Europeans, hence the term "savage." This would somehow make the land taking, in the minds of Europeans of the time, less immoral.

Settlers introduced plowing, single-crop farming, dam construction, organized animal husbandry, and many other practices viewed as destructive by the tribes. All these practices, plus the continuing efforts at colonial expansion, caused enough friction that war finally broke out in 1622. In just a few hours, 350 to 400 colonists were slaughtered—a third of the total English population in the area. The attack, led by Opechancanough, a successor of Chief Powhatan's, defined what the power struggle between Indians and non-Indians would become in the next three centuries: war—until one of the two cultures prevailed.

Several warring and trade alliances were established and dissolved across the eastern seaboard as more and more settlements were established. The Dutch arrived to join the other European powers in the bonanza that the continent would clearly become. In 1626, they purchased Manhattan Island from the Indians of the same name.

Colonial settlement was made easier by the fact that tribes were not united. Some would fight on the side of the colonists against other tribes, or against another colonial power. In New

England, the Mohicans allied themselves with the British against the Pequots, who were routed in the Pequot War of 1637.

As early as 1645, some colonists and missionaries were openly expressing their opinion that there was something wrong with the way the colonial powers were treating the previous occupants of the land. The Indians, wrote a Jesuit missionary, were "hardly barbarous, save in name," and had a "marvelous faculty for remembering places, and for describing them to one another." Views on the treatment of Indians followed a pattern: to most of those who lived on the expanding frontier, Indians were dangerous savages that had to be dealt with by using force. To those who lived in Europe or in New World towns, where whites were a majority, the idea of the Noble Red Man developed. Proximity was the key.

The first town for Christianized Indians, writes Paula Mitchell Marks, was established in 1646. A missionary was usually in charge, providing a mixture of religious and autocratic rule. Indians who came to live in these early versions of reservations did so for protection and a sense of security. It was a high price to pay since, once a resident of these "praying towns," it was nearly impossible to retain Indian ways. All of the laws that had to be observed had the goal of "civilizing" the residents. Indians who refused to join the new communities slowly lost their self-sufficiency by becoming dependent on the items that trade with the colonists provided. Indian men began to spend most of their time trapping, with the women cleaning and tanning the furs for delivery to European traders. They had less and less time for hunting and gathering food. The important thing was to produce enough trade in order to acquire European goods, alcohol being one of them.

Trade with the Europeans completely changed the social structure of some tribes. Material possessions developed new standards of social status among Indians. The feeling of community began to fall apart. Tribes began to compete with one another for the dwindling supply of fur and other natural resources. And without furs, the tribes had to pay for European goods with their land.

So another war had to come to relieve the pressure that had so far accumulated, and it came in 1675, in the form of King Philip's War. King Philip was not an Englishman but a Pokunoket chief whose real name was Metacom. In fourteen months, he led several bands in the destruction of twelve frontier settlements. His was the last major act of war against the colonists of southern New England. It failed in good part because the Mohegan, Pequot, Massachusetts, and Nauset Indians fought on the side of the English.

King Philip's War is a good example of how important alliances were in the fight over final control of the continent. Indian tribes were not a homogenous group. Several tribes, like some of the colonists themselves, were only interested in dominating the land. All those fighting for dominance would do whatever it took to attain it. The eighteenth and nineteenth centuries saw Europeans succeed.

Establishing the U.S.A.

(The Lower 48)

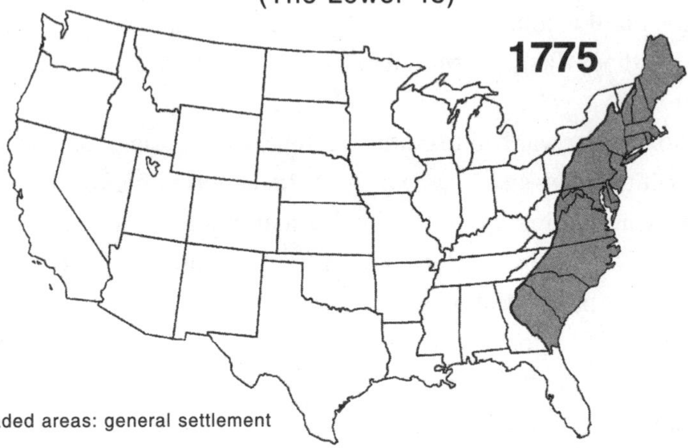

Shaded areas: general settlement

Below: cities or towns founded, adopted, settled, or established by non-Indians during the same period.

1701	Detroit, MI	1739	Memphis, TN
1706	Albuquerque, NM	1754	Pittsburgh, PA
1718	San Antonio, TX	1762	Charlotte, NC
1718	New Orleans, LA	1764	St. Louis, MO
1729	Baltimore, MD		

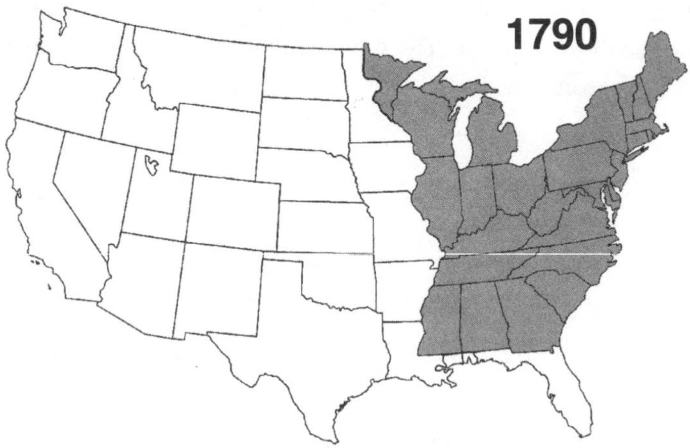

1776	Tucson, AZ	1779	Nashville, TN
1777	San Jose, CA	1779	Chicago, IL
1778	1st U.S.-Indian treaty	1781	Los Angeles, CA

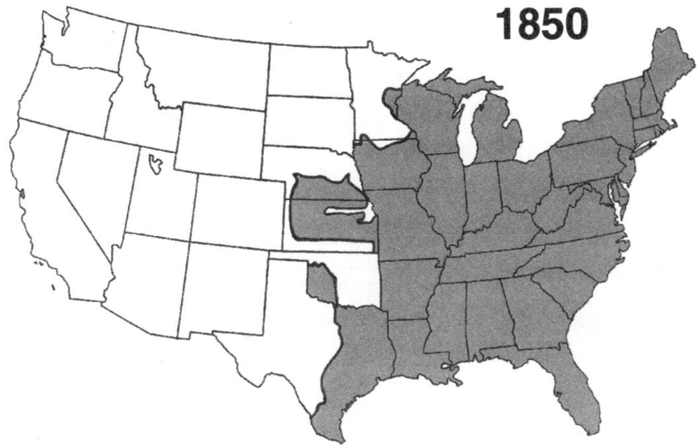

1795 Milwaukee, WI
1795 Cleveland, OH
1804 Omaha, NE
1812 Columbus, OH
1819 Minneapolis, MN
1820 Oakland, CA
1820 Indianapolis, IN
1832 Toledo, OH
1835 Austin, TX
1836 Miami, FL
1836 Houston, TX
1836 Atlanta, GA
1839 Sacramento, CA
1841 Dallas, TX
1846 San Francisco, CA
1849 Fort Worth, TX
1850 Kansas City, MO

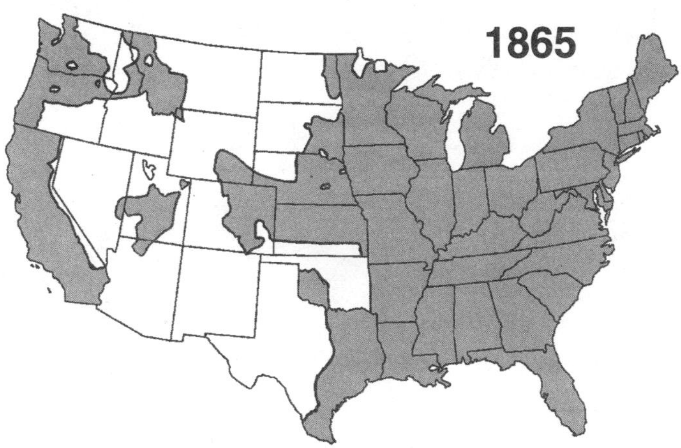

1851 Seattle, WA
1859 Denver, CO
1864 Phoenix, AZ

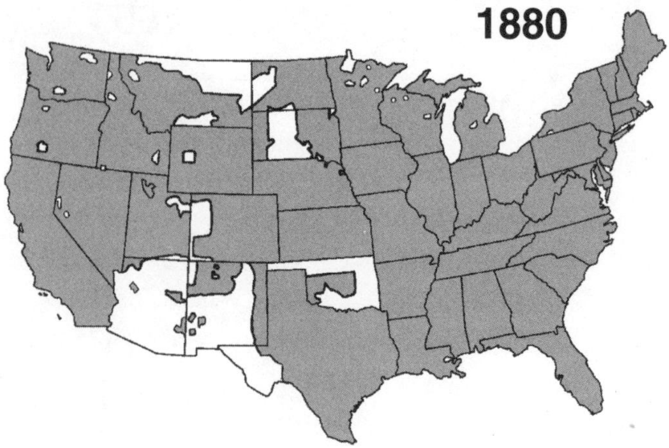

1872 Fresno, CA

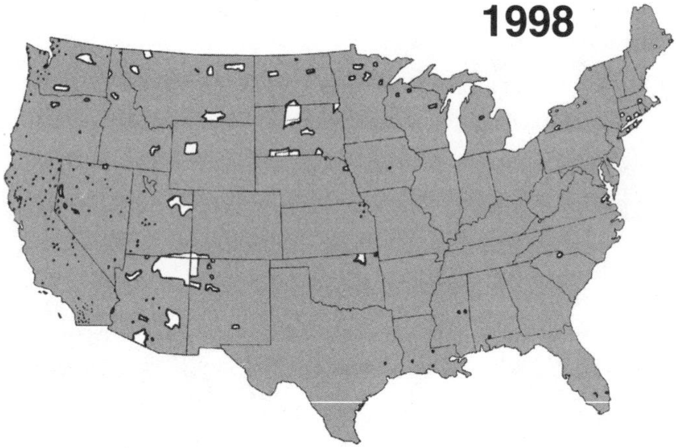

1884 Portland, OR

1889 Oklahoma City, OK

Smallpox

It has been called the first use of biological warfare—armies of whites passing out infected blankets and handkerchiefs to Indians. It has also been called the reason Europeans were able to prevail over Indians. Without microbes, the early wars may have had a different outcome. In fact, in the case of New England, at least, the Indian population had already been badly affected by smallpox before the arrival of the Pilgrims in 1620.

Ordinary reports about the effects of the disease are much more illuminating than any speculation about secret attempts at biological warfare. On 30 July 1837, a Mandan warrior gave a speech about a smallpox outbreak at Fort Clark, North Dakota: "Ever since I can remember," he said, "I have loved the Whites...and to the best of my knowledge, I have never wronged a white man....Listen well what I have to say, as it will be the last time you will hear me. Think of your wives, children, brothers, sisters, friends, and in fact all that you hold dear, are all dead, or dying, with their faces all rotten, caused by those dogs the whites, think of all that, my friends, and rise all together and not leave one of them alive...."

Francis Chardon, the fur trapper in charge of the Fort Clark trading post, wrote a day-to-day account of how the epidemic progressed, and how it was accompanied by threats against whites. It is a very impartial narrative, with no trace of antipathy toward the Indians:

"[5 August 1837] News from the Gros Ventres...many of them have died of the small pox—several chiefs among them. They swear revenge against all the whites, as they say the small pox was brought here by the steamboat....[8 August] Seven more died today....[15 August] The Mandans went up to the Gros Ventres with a pipe, to make them smoke, to try to get them to help murder us; the Gros Ventres refused to smoke with them, saying that they were friendly to the whites and that they would not take part with them....[19 August] I was in hopes that the disease was almost at an end, but they are dying off 8 and 10 every day—and new cases of it daily—where it will stop, God only Knows....A young Ree that has been sick for some time with the small pox, and being alone in his lodge, thought that it was better to die than to be in so much pain, he began to rub the scabs until blood was running all over his body, he rolled himself in the ashes, which almost burnt his soul out of his body—two days after he was perfectly well, it is a severe operation, but few are disposed to try it—however, it proved beneficial to him."

Chardon caught the disease himself. As medication, he took "hot whiskey punch...which made me sweat all last night, this Morning I took my daily bitters as usual." His most powerful descriptions are reserved for how Indians dealt with the disease: "An Indian vaccinated his child by cutting two small pieces of flesh out of his arms, and two on the belly—and then taking a scab from one that was getting well of the disease, and rubbing it on the wounded part. Three days after, it took effect, and the child is perfectly well....The number of deaths up to the present is very near five hundred...."

Smallpox was not easily controlled in colonial America. Even as late as 1958, the annual death toll from smallpox in the world was at two million people. The last known, naturally occurring outbreak of smallpox took place in Somalia, in October of 1977, according to Dr. Alan Cann of the University of Leicester, England.

Intermarriage

It is unfortunate that intermarriage between Indians and colonists was forbidden in many of the English colonies. In the

French and Spanish colonies, although not openly encouraged, intermarriage became an important means of integration for the various cultures involved. Magnus Mörner writes in *Race Mixture in the History of Latin America* that "no part of the world has ever witnessed such a gigantic mixing of races as the one that has been taking place in Latin America and the Caribbean since 1492."

English colonists did not participate in part because of feelings of racial superiority. Another reason was the fact that English settlers were farmers, for the most part. They believed that a farming household required the technical skills of European women.

The Inevitable

Once enough Europeans had arrived, with no immigration policy to stop more from coming, it was inevitable that land would become an issue of contention. Aside from experiencing drastic changes in social and environmental conditions, Indians often had to deal with the most merciless colonists—the ones most likely to be the point men of the colonizing effort. Natives were forced to compete not only with Europeans but with each other. They were unable to form or maintain a cohesive force with which to face the threat of losing their lands and cultures.

It would require a great deal of imagination to visualize what it must feel like to see thousands of strangers arrive—and stay—uninvited. Hollywood tries to lend a hand: In the popular 1996 movie *Independence Day*, space aliens, with what is obviously new technology, begin to destroy human civilization with sudden attacks. Being a Hollywood release, the movie has a happy ending, even after several major cities in the world are destroyed and millions of humans die. When the alien invasion begins, the realization that nothing like it has ever been seen before—that the invaders are inexplicably powerful—is followed by panic. Such must have been the experience of many Indians when Europeans were populating their land.

The pace of the invasion of the Americas was not as swift as the one depicted in the movie, but slowly a new structure emerged. Less than a century after the founding of Jamestown, life had changed permanently for the tribes that had been in contact with colonists. There was no going back. To try to do so was not only irrational but impossible.

The Need For Treaties

The new arrivals had the most to gain from treaty-making. The tribes had already lost much of their domain and agreed to the signing of treaties knowing that continuing the fight would only mean death. After the War of 1812, the United States had little need for military alliances with Indian tribes against the British. With the use of treaties, twelve more states joined the Union in the four decades that followed.

In expanding the young nation, the United States government tried to acquire land from the Indians in what was viewed as the most moral way possible: by purchasing it. Many of the emerging nations in Latin America simply took the land from the natives. Those nations did not have "the sense of morality of the United States," as put by Native American scholar Vine Deloria, Jr.

This sense of morality was not perfect, of course. There were many abuses, lies, and empty promises involved. So it pays to keep in mind the goal the U.S. had in signing the treaties: to facilitate white settlement. This is best illustrated by the fact that throughout the country's history, several treaties were upheld only when it was convenient to the federal government. Morality aside, that is the prerogative of a military victor and the result of any successful invasion. The dominant force—the new ruler—adjusts the laws of the land to what it feels is best for the purpose of its own survival. "Even as the last treaties were being written," notes John Collier, "white men were moving in and over lands reserved to Indians, and the government was quick to back up white claims to land it had only recently set aside as Indian land."

Why should it be any different? What else can anyone expect from an invasion? Even Vine Deloria, Jr., has stated that "Treaties are made to be broken" (although he maintains that property-conveyance treaties are "holy writs"). If vast armies of Europeans had arrived heavily armed in 1492, with the *specific* purpose of a scorched-earth campaign, the event would earn the historical category of war. Such a campaign, if sustained, would have eventually exterminated all groups then living on the continent. The difference here is that colonists arrived peacefully, for the most part, and made a poor effort at incorporating those already here into the dominant system they brought with them. That effort is still going on today, badly managed and lacking in all manner of common sense.

By the late 1860s, many in Congress felt that the use of treaties was a hopelessly obsolete practice. They did so because treaties made "nations" out of Indian tribes that were anything but. In other words, the phoniness of treaties was too plain and not in tune with the goals of the U.S. Constitution. Treaties were not helping the Indian, either. Tribal economies were a disaster. Reservations were turning into cesspools of poverty. With the Civil War over, there was a need to take new steps toward including Indians in the development of the country. In addition, thanks to annuities and other payments, treaties were becoming prohibitively expensive. So an effort began to replace tribal ownership of land by allotment to individual Indians.

From 1871 on, treaties were replaced by "agreements" and "special laws" passed to handle the special relationship between the U.S. government and Indian tribes. This new approach made little difference: Congress has never understood that what's really needed is an end to the "special relationship" with Indian tribes, and to the corruption, abuses and bureaucracy that go with it.

Native sovereignty nationalists insist that the U.S. has violated most treaties and that very few tribes would have signed them had they known that things would turn out this way. This is unlikely. It was obvious from very early on that the U.S. would demand signing new treaties whenever it felt it was necessary to change the rules to acquire more land. Tribes signed the treaties because, in war, they had no choice. They might have won the war if they had decimated the first colonists, but that did not happen. Militarily speaking, it was a tactical mistake, and the tribes paid the consequences.

"The promises of self-government found in a multitude of treaties," writes Deloria, Jr., "the promises of protection by the United States from wrongs committed by its citizens, the promises that the tribes would be respected as nations on whose behalf the United States acted as a trustee before the eyes of the world, were all vital parts of the treaty rights which Indians believe they have received from the United States."

The reality is that treaties were never of any use to American Indians because droves of whites kept on coming back to haunt them. The more immigration there was, the more treaties and removals and broken promises. (Treaties were also meaningless if the U.S. Cavalry decided to declare a tribe "hostile" and subject to military action.) This was not planned as such. It just happened.

Why was there such a wave of migration to America? The new country promised economic opportunity and equal treatment under the law—both very powerful magnets.

By the time the United States ended the practice of signing treaties, it found itself holding millions of acres of land in trust for the tribes. In the view of landless new arrivals to the country, that land was not being used productively. They wanted the government to turn the trust lands into homesteads. "The trick," write's Deloria, Jr., "was to get at the Indian [trust] lands in such a manner as to make it appear as if the government was helping the Indians, not taking their lands once again."

Allotment and Reversals

In *From Every Zenith*, John Collier asks: "How could the treaties be scrapped without laying the basis for Indian claims against the Treasury? The land allotment system was the answer."

Jesse Chisholm had established a cattle route in 1866 through what became the Oklahoma Territory. The route became known as the Chisholm Trail, and the non-Indians who used it began to pressure the U.S. government to allow settlement along it. Once that happened, the land rush was unbelievable. When Oklahoma was officially organized as a territory on 2 May 1890, there were about 60,000 non-Indians living on it. Ten years later, the number had increased to 400,000. In part, this was due to the fear by whites that other whites would do the same before them. Settlers were competing to claim "the best lands."

Non-Indians were not the only ones getting land through the allotment process, however. The purpose of allotment was to create a system of individual land ownership for everyone. At first, each Indian family was given an average of 160 acres for the head of household, plus 80 acres to others in the family over eighteen years of age. Today we are told that the amount of land allotted was not sufficient to support Indian families, that once a generation died and the land was passed on to the next generation, it had to be divided among all surviving children, then all the grandchildren, and so on, until, after a few generations, there was no land left to inherit.

Subsequent generations of the original non-Indian settlers were also liable to inherit no land if they had kept on dividing the property equally among all children every time someone died. The difference is that they didn't.

The General Allotment (or Dawes) Act of 1887 was an effort to establish this American system of land ownership among Indian tribes. "There is little question that the leadership for passage of the Dawes Act came from those sympathetic to the Indians," writes William C. Canby, Jr. "They believed that if individual Indians were given plots of land to cultivate, they would prosper and become assimilated into the mainstream of American culture as middle-class farmers." Things did not turn out that way. After a twenty-five-year period in which the new individual Indian landowners were exempt from state property taxes, many could not earn enough to hold their lands and were forced to sell them. Indian culture suffered a heavy blow. "Banished was the Indian social heritage,…" writes Collier, "the language, and the traditional religious observances."

Allotment had seemed like a fair—or at least sensible—solution. But instead of giving it time to show positive results, Indian sympathizers decided to intervene again with a complete reversal of their allotment policy. The results were even more disastrous, proving that in the history of the United States, there has been no worst enemy to the American Indian than those who are purportedly "pro" Indian.

When John Collier was Commissioner of Indian Affairs in the early 1930s, he had plans to become the Bartolomé de Las Casas of the twentieth century, helping not only United States Indians but Indigenous peoples everywhere in the world.

In the U.S., Collier's policies had three chief objectives:

- Rehabilitating the Indian economy on the reservation.
- Organizing self-government for all Indian tribes.
- Establishing opportunities for Indian civil and cultural freedom.

In other words, an end to allotment and a total return to a past that was long gone. The Meriam Report—a study of the social and economic conditions of American Indians—had generated enough white guilt in the early 1930s to pass, with the dexterous hand of John Collier's leadership, the Congressional bill that eventually became the Indian Reorganization Act (IRA) of 1934—a monumental step back.

In what almost seems like a tragicomedy, Federal Indian Policy continued to flip-flop in the decades that followed. The IRA was doomed to be a failure because it went in the exact opposite direction of the Constitution's Fourteenth Amendment, despite Franklin Delano Roosevelt's Indian New Deal's proposal to "grant Indians the same legal rights enjoyed by other Americans…." The IRA had little to do with "same."

After World War II, say the authors of *The Native Americans: An Illustrated History*, "Americans cherished the illusion of a happy, homogeneous America devoid of serious racial or cultural divisions." It was not an illusion but an effort to include everyone and hopefully avoid the horrific results brought on in Europe during the war, when the Nazis had made different treatment of citizens under the law an official policy.

The Indian Claims Commission (ICC) and Termination were an overt effort to homogenize the American population for the sake of stability and adherence to the U.S. Constitution. The ICC allowed Indians to file claims and receive payments for past losses and settle all grievances with finality. Termination was meant to dissolve all reservations and—through Public Law 280—finally allow the states to have jurisdiction over Indian lands within their borders.

Urban integration of the Indian was seen as a key in this process. After World War II, Indians participated in relocation programs that included urban housing, assistance and training—much like the programs offered to those European immigrants who were starting new lives in the United States during and after the war. Cities like Denver, Minneapolis, Chicago and Los Angeles became magnets for the newly urbanized Native American. After termination, Indians were no longer to be considered Indian by any government—local, state, or federal—and Congress would be free from its "trust relationship" and responsibilities to Indians of the past. The parent-child relationship was to end. The "Great Father," as tribes used to call the President of the United States, could not be responsible for his children forever. They had to take care of themselves.

The Menominee tribe of Wisconsin completed its termination process in December of 1961. For some strange reason, the Menominee termination plan included turning the tribe into a corporation—Menominee Enterprises, Inc.—and its members into "shareholders." This only perpetuated the communal ownership, and Congress set several restrictions on what this "corporation" could do, restrictions that didn't apply to any other corporation. The insidious role of government was at play again, saying, "Yes, we want you to be like all other Americans, but you can't do this, and this, and that."

On the other hand, Menominee termination meant no more "protection and services." Protection from taxation, and free services like health, education, and utilities. "Individual Menominee were forced to pay for electricity and water that they previously received at no cost," complained an anti-termination advocacy group. Such free services, in the eyes of Native sovereignty nationalists, are a birthright and a permanent entitlement for tribal members.

We would all be upset if—after having lived all our lives in a socialist structure where all services are free and everything is done for us—we suddenly found ourselves left to our own devices, and with some patronizing figure telling us what to do and what not to do with our resources. In good part because of U.S. government interference (the Menominees were not allowed to take out mortgages on their own property, for example), termination plunged the tribe into administrative chaos and growing poverty. It wasn't long before the tribe began clamoring for restoration of the Menominee Reservation and a return to the special trust relationship it had enjoyed with the United States. Led by tribal activist Ada Deer, the Menominee sought the protection and services of the Great Father once more, like a failed adult-child going back to live with his parents.

The special perks enjoyed by Native Americans—the "protection and services" mentioned above—are considered a birthright because of the idea that Indians were here first, and that they are entitled to permanent payment for the land they lost to non-Indians. This type of thinking is not unique to the United States. Indonesia has a similar situation with two different ethnic groups—the Dayak and the Madurese.

The Dayak were there first and considered "savages" in the nineteenth century. "For thousands of years, before the arrival of the Dutch and the British, the Dayaks dominated Borneo," writes Richard Lloyd Parry in *Granta*. This sounds very much like the Native American contention that "we were here for thousands and thousands of years. This is our land." It all changed for the Dayak in 1945, when tribal members became full citizens of the

Republic of Indonesia. Even their cannibalism (eating their enemies) came to a stop.

Today, the Madurese are moving in and the Dayak don't like it. Indonesia is fast approaching the population size of the United States, on land that is roughly twenty percent the size of our fifty combined states. Instead of fifty states, however, they have 17,000 islands, many of them too small to be of any use.

With the help of the World Bank, the Indonesian government has set in motion a program to relocate up to sixty-five million citizens from some highly populated islands (like Java) to others less so, "at the expense of indigenous groups like the Dayaks and their traditional way of life," writes Parry.

Here we run into this "traditional way of life" business again. It should be obvious that such a thing cannot be sustained in this day and age. Traditional ways of life were doomed the moment the industrial revolution began over a century ago. We can be as outraged about it as we please, but as long as humans continue to be consumers of modern technology, there will be incentive for industrial development. Industrial development means income to many people. Income means expansion, constant change. Native sovereignty nationalists don't want to go back to living in the stereotypical tepee, or to roaming the range. So what does it mean to retain a traditional way of life?

Resistance to change in Indonesia has generated a tremendous amount of violence (cannibalism among the Dayak is back). It is worth noting that the 1974 Indian Declaration of Independence in the United States was not followed by an armed struggle to rid Indian "nations" of the white man's yoke. There has been no war in America because there is no will among American Indians to restore "traditional ways of life." It is only Native sovereignty nationalists who are still making the demands, the only ones who refuse to accept the fact that the traditional is no longer here. As the only likely beneficiaries, they are the small minority still pushing for Indian nationhood while the rest of America lets them stir.

Impossible Demand

In the early 1970s, Sol Tax, a professor of anthropology at the University of Chicago, made this proposal: "With our growing urbanization, we are vacating again almost the whole of the continent. We no longer 'need' all that land, and are only misusing it as we once misused the people who treated it as sacred....To accomplish tribal autonomy requires that we begin with it and ask them, tribe by tribe, how we should replace some of the assets which once made it possible for tribes to live."

Mr. Tax provides a list of what he believes Native Americans' wishes to be. These include turning over all "unused" federal lands to tribes, "tax-free and in irrevocable trust," and providing American Indians, in perpetuity and through a trust fund, "such services as health, education and welfare."

But we have a model of government that doesn't call for all this. Although it isn't perfect, it works well most of the time, and it has realistic and achievable goals. If we don't like the goals, we can try to change them by following the procedures set forth by the Founders. If for any reason tyranny keeps us from changing them, then the system is corrupt and must be overthrown.

Native sovereignty nationalists have claimed for years that the American system is a tyranny. But they have never had the support to overthrow it because their claim is not supported by relevant evidence. Nevertheless, sovereignty nationalists have gone through the motions of beginning a revolution to overthrow the system. The Twenty Points and the Native American Declaration of Independence in the early 1970s were initiatives toward that end. But they came to nothing because they had no reason to exist. They received no support, even from Native Americans, and were considered little more than the publicity stunts and gimmickry they obviously were—fifteen minutes of fame for the few Native sovereignty nationalists promoting them.

For better or worse, the territory that was once ruled by hundreds of scattered tribes—themselves the descendants of ancient immigrants from Asia, as far as it is known—is now ruled by some 270 million Americans, all of whom should expect nothing less from the current form of government than equal treatment under the law for all: One country, one law.

Unavoidable Assimilation

No One Noticed

Assimilation has already taken place. As a result, those who believe that assimilation is wrong equate the word "assimilation" to the word "genocide." To them, assimilation implies being swallowed, overwhelmed and destroyed by surrounding cultures. But this is not what has happened or should happen to Native American cultures.

The current force behind assimilation is our information revolution and the social structures it has ushered in. Whites, blacks, Indians—all races and cultures—assimilate by default to this powerful force. Those who refuse to, do so at the risk of ending up paupers (and their cultures wiped out via economic failure). Everyone is subject to this rule of modernity, not just Native Americans.

The information revolution is separate from culture. It has nothing to do with it. Various types of music, food, and dance will continue to exist. Core tastes will remain. But more and more, cultures *will* merge. Education will not be able to act independently from this merging force. A child born today who refuses, as she grows up, to learn to use computers, will not survive economically as an adult. When Johann Gutenberg came up with a movable-type printing press, the world was forced to assimilate to that new form of information technology. Prior to Gutenberg, thousands of monks had been engaged in copying books by hand. An industrious monk copied between 1,200 to 1,300 pages a year. Fifty years after Gutenberg, writes Peter Drucker in *Forbes ASAP*, "the monks had become unemployed. These monks (some estimates go well above 10,000 for all of Europe) had been replaced by a very small number of lay craftsmen, the newly minted class of 'printers,' totaling perhaps 1,000....By 1580 or so, the printers, with their focus on technology, had become ordinary craftsmen...their place was soon taken by what we now call publishers."

Today, the Federal Bureau of Labor Statistics' *Occupational Outlook Handbook* is forecasting fifty million new jobs in the next seven years. This estimate represents a fourteen percent increase over 1996 numbers. But the job outlook "is bleak for people who do not acquire specialized skills (farm workers, down nine percent, for example), or cannot adapt to technological change (telephone operators, down nine percent)," writes Brad Edmondson in *Utne Reader*. Farm workers and telephone operators will have to adapt. They have no choice.

Indian leaders of over one hundred years ago recognized this. The Sioux, like most other tribes, knew that a growing dependence on the awls, axes, knives, blankets, and rations the government had promised through treaties meant the end of their native way of life and the beginning of assimilation.

Red Cloud, the Oglala Sioux chief, said regarding the tribe's position when it had first made treaties with the United States: "Our old life and our old customs were about to end; the game upon which we lived was disappearing; the whites were closing around us, and nothing remained for us but to adopt their ways and have the same rights with them if we wished to save ourselves."

Everyone participates in assimilation, not just minorities. The majority also assimilates to the constantly changing social structure of a growing population. The white population of the United States dropped ten percent (as a percentage of the total) between 1970 and 1990. The "Hispanic" population doubled. Asians and other "non-white" Americans tripled.

Myths

It seems stupid to even say it, but American Indians no longer live in tepees or wigwams or other traditional dwellings. A large number of them may still belong to the poorer segments of the population, but poverty has not kept them from assimilating. Electricity is widely used on reservations. Indian households have radios, televisions and cars. Every American has gone through the same process of technological adaptation.

The idea that all Native Americans once lived in tepees is as much part of a myth as is the idea that all Indians were hunters. Before 1492, the continent was home to tribes that used very different social structures and were at various stages of technological development. Most Indians were farmers, not hunters.

By the time the Cherokee were forced to move to "Indian Territory," they had a constitution, owned slaves, and published their own newspapers. A census of the Cherokee, taken some twelve years before removal, showed them owning 2,923 plows, 2,566 sheep, 46,732 swine, 22,531 cattle, 7,683 horses, 33 grist mills, 13 saw mills, 69 blacksmith shops, 762 looms, 2,486 spinning wheels, 2 tan yards, 172 wagons. These possessions are not part of the infrastructure of a hunting and gathering society.

Today, there is a tendency to insist that assimilation has not taken place and will never do so, despite the increasing number of Indians attending state universities and earning something as "white" as a law degree. In the past thirty years, the number of Native American lawyers has increased one-hundred fold.

"When they graduate," writes Scott Baldauf in *The Christian Science Monitor*, "many of [the University of New Mexico's] 'legal warriors' head off for the reservations, where they serve as tribal attorneys or judges. Others work for law firms that represent tribes or federal or state government agencies that deal with Indian issues." Law is a profession close to the power structure of the United States. Tribal law is not. And though many of the young "legal warriors" end up working in tribal courts, their legal foundation rests on degrees earned at state universities.

It takes a few minutes of browsing the Internet's World Wide Web to see how adapted American Indian tribes are to this recent form of communication technology. In November of 1998, a firm named FutureNet Online, Inc., announced an "E-Commerce Cyberstore" in association with the Lake Superior Chippewa Indians. Their business plan was to "penetrate and serve the vast Native American Markets through Internet shopping," according to *Business Wire*.

Kevin Maulson, a member of the Lac du Flambeau Band of Chippewa, was named the Chief Executive Officer of The Trading Post Cyberstore. "Tribal members will have the opportunity," he said, "to shop from Worldwide's Buy-It-All mall which in the very near future will offer several millions of products." Shoppers on the reservation were expected to access the Cyberstore through WebTV, a box that is set on television sets, much like cable boxes. According to the report, Tom Maulson, the tribe's Chairman, had participated in the donation of WebTV boxes and keyboards to the Lac du Flambeau by an organization called Computers for Kids a few months earlier. The donor was an affiliate of FutureNet Online, Inc.

The Seminole Tribe has a well-designed, very professional Internet Site (www.seminoletribe.com), as do many other tribes.

Online newspapers like the *Seminole Tribune* are not the product of people who have not assimilated.

Modern-day casinos are marvels of technological gadgetry. Many of them may be built and run by professionals hired by the tribes, but mere ownership and contact with the gaming industry is no less a form of assimilation than attending state universities to earn law or medical degrees.

Real Culture

American Indian culture will survive because American culture will keep it alive. There is tremendous interest in Native American crafts, music, foods, and mysticism. Granted, much of it is driven by crass commercialism, but the same has happened to other celebrations of culture. Renaissance Festivals, St. Patrick's Day, Oktoberfest—they have all become commercialized while being adopted by the American mainstream.

You don't have to be Irish to celebrate St. Patrick's Day in America. Native Americanness can also be a part of being American if Federal Indian Policy were not doing its darndest to induce resentment between the cultures by treating each differently under the law.

The Native American culture of tomorrow will not be like today's, nor like that of the past. All cultures die at some point. They are replaced by new developments. The culture of the genuine Victorian gentleman is as much history as is that of the virtuous, proud Indian chief of the 1800s, or of the oppressed, antebellum black slave.

Writing about Northern Ireland in *The New Yorker*, Fintan O'Toole describes culture as "the shape a place takes when it's inside the heads of its peoples: all the habits, attitudes, and values they take for granted....Culture is how you see yourself. In divided societies, culture is also how other people see you."

Whatever divisions exist now, they will be slowly erased. In the adapt-or-perish atmosphere of modern societies, stereotypes are taken over by more powerful cultural forces. "Television and shopping,..." writes O'Toole, "have seeped into everybody's soul." The World Tourism Organization has put the number of people who travel from one country to another every year at six hundred million. That is more than twice the population of the United States—people going from one place to another, being exposed to different cultures and forcing, with their tourism, a general globalization of culture. The number of such travelers is expected to surpass one billion within the next ten years. This may be considered a sad development by many—the fact that almost a sixth of the world's population is able to afford a trip abroad—but it is reality.

The amazing feat of the American experience is to have established a world power out of the disparate groups of nationalists and separatists who inhabited the land at the time of Independence. English colonists came to desire complete separation from England. European immigrants, at least until the end of World War II, tended to sever their connections with the Old World. American Indians tried their best to keep their distance from the encroaching Europeans.

Today, the ideal of integration seems to be fading, even as technology is pushing the other way. People are said to want to go back to their "roots," to separate. Native Americans, we are told, must have their sovereignty. Homeschoolers, religious groups, militiamen, neo-Luddites, and various ethnic groups want to establish their own surreal cocoons. But the consequence of "continuously emphasizing difference," writes Gerald Early in *Civilization*, "is to make difference the only reality.... Multiculturalism has made it nearly impossible to talk about human difference except to deplore any discomfort we have with it. The effect of multiculturalism is to make people feel more different than they actually are."

The Tricksters

Philip J. Deloria uses the Native American trickster tale tradition as an analogy for Native American non-participation in mainstream American society. The trickster is a mythical figure, usually male, who is part human and part animal. He is often an amoral and comic troublemaker.

Deloria implies that Native Americans have never been part of American culture. Since the first contact with Europeans, they have moved among the white man as "trickster people," not as themselves—sort of like wearing a mask whenever there's a white man around. "Indians have lived the twentieth century…" he writes, becoming "the Other" (i.e., "white" on the outside) while remaining themselves. This is quite an achievement. Was Goyathlay (a.k.a. Geronimo) being a trickster when he became a Dutch Reformed Christian? Was he being a trickster when he participated in President Theodore Roosevelt's 1905 inaugural? And how about Senator Ben Nighthorse Campbell of Colorado today—is he just wearing a mask every day he spends on Capitol Hill?

Deloria believes that white Americans have "eagerly erected" boundaries of "us" and "them" between the two cultures. But only those clamoring for different treatment under the law can be said to be engaged in an us-and-them game today.

Things haven't changed much in the last quarter century of Federal Indian Policy. In 1974 the federal government was spending almost a billion dollars a year on "Indian problems," much of it by funding that bureaucratic juggernaut—the Bureau of Indian Affairs. (Fiscal 1999 appropriations for the BIA and Indian Health Service alone were almost four billion dollars.) "Instead of preparing Indians to confront the modern world," writes scholar Vine Deloria, Jr., the Bureau spent its money training "yet another generation of bureaucrats to handle the affairs of Indians." Here, Vine Deloria, Jr., seems to accept the reality of assimilation. What does "preparing Indians to confront the modern world" mean if not assimilation?

Responsibilities

A good reason to refuse to admit that Native American culture has already blended into American culture is that doing so would undermine the demand for continued government set-asides and special programs designed only for tribal members. These programs and economic assistance take the tone of a demand when they are called "responsibilities" of the federal government.

Overt calls for responsibility began in 1961 with a national Indian conference that was "restricted to Indians, whites being permitted as silent observers at some of the open sessions," according to historian Virgil Vogel. Sixty-four tribes were represented at the conference, and they produced documents with titles such as "Declaration of Indian Purpose" and "What Indians Want."

These documents admitted, even then, that change was inevitable: "The conditions in which Indians live today reflect a world in which every basic aspect of life has been transformed. Even the physical world is no longer the controlling factor in determining where and under what conditions men may live....These changes were followed by major shifts in the internal life of tribe and family. The time came when the Indian people were no longer the masters of their situation."

Because the United States is responsible for the drastic changes imposed on the tribes, it has a moral responsibility, the Declaration said, to answer to Indian people: "Our situation cannot be relieved by appropriated funds alone, though it is equally obvious that without capital investment and funded services, solutions will be delayed. Nor will the passage of time lessen the complexities which beset a people moving toward new meaning and purpose."

We must remember that this was in 1961. Are tribes still "moving toward new meaning and purpose" at the end of the twentieth century?

"What we ask of America," the Declaration said, "is not charity, not paternalism, even when benevolent....In short, the Indians ask for assistance, technical and financial, *for the time needed, however long that may be*." [Emphasis added.]

How long must the United States allow Native sovereignty nationalists to manipulate the system by claiming that assimilation is simply not possible and, therefore, American taxpayers must perpetually pay for tribal health, education, housing, and other community services? How long is long enough?

Apparently never. Columnist Tim Giago, the Lakota Sioux editor and publisher of *Indian Country Today*, says that "Indian nations gave up millions of acres of land for perpetual funds to educate their children, for health care and other rights, and for the right to run their own governments."

If "perpetual funds" were indeed offered, they were perpetual only to those who offered them. An individual—and a nation of individuals—cannot promise that his children and grandchildren will support someone else's children and grandchildren, and so on, forever. He has no right to make such a promise.

The United States will never achieve equal treatment for all its citizens under the law as long as it professes to have "responsibilities" to only a small segment of the population.

Language

In the matter of language, the government is also said to have a responsibility to keep every Indian language alive, even when there are no longer any native speakers of a given language. Only a handful of the 200 North American Indian languages have more than 1,000 speakers. When Red Thunder Cloud, the last known speaker of Catawba, died in early 1996, demands for an organized effort to "save the languages" soon began to take shape.

But it is not the role of government to preserve languages. If no one is interested enough to privately support a grammatical structure and the vocabulary and culture that go with it, then the language should die. Permanent life support may give some scholar the excuse for a profession and keep the grants coming, but the grants should come from private donations and not be tax deductible.

In addition, there is nothing more socially limiting to a child than to have a personal language instructor at school to help her "gain familiarity" with her tribe's native tongue. It is the parents' job to do that, not the taxpayers' via school programs. Those who want a given language to survive should pay for it.

Language "genocide" is not taking place solely in North America. Estimates state that at least half of the existing languages in the world (some 6,000) will be gone in a century. Scholars mourn this. They may have the time and funds to pursue preserving those languages, but government should quit having the messianic tendency to save and "preserve" everything. There is simply no time in the human dimension to do so. We don't get up every morning and say, "Today, I'm going to work toward saving the Basque and Welsh languages, feed all the poor in Africa and educate them until they are self-sufficient, ecologically-adept human beings. I'll work with human-rights activists to do away with tyranny and oppression everywhere, do away with greed and economic exploitation of the poor by the rich, fight for animal rights, save the manatee from extinction…" The list would never end.

We can talk all we want about culture, but the definition of culture today is "that which makes humans survive." In our modern world, human survival is intrinsically tied to economic survival. If you don't speak the language of currency, your chances are largely diminished. Children may do well learning an obscure, ancestral tongue at home. But once school attendance begins, it makes the most economic (and common) sense to learn the dominant language of the land, and learn it well.

In the case of Welsh, for example, once a youngster has learned the English term "Public Footpath" at school, why should anyone expect him to use the Welsh *Llwybr Cyhoeddus*, which less than twenty percent of the Welsh population understands? To the mind of someone who is learning the more popular language (English), "Llwybr Cyhoeddus" needlessly complicates things and, most of all, is useless if Welsh has been declining as a language during the last two decades. Is reality a bad thing? The Welsh may not want to admit this, but very few people outside Wales will bother to learn their language. Barring an invasion and occupation of all of Europe by mighty Welsh forces capable of controlling laws and commerce, "Llwybr Cyhoeddus" is not going anywhere.

The Basque language offers a similar situation. While the Basque government is bent on forcing the population of the Basque Country in northern Spain (most of it not Basque) to learn the language, students go through the motions—they "learn" what is required of them in order to graduate from high school, and then quickly forget the *Euskaltzaindia*s and the *artzai txakurrak*s and go on to use the only language that allows them to survive economically in Spain: Spanish.

Human communication is seeing a revolution. We can't expect all languages and cultures to survive. Because of the Internet and international trade, English is spoken by more people in the world than any other in history. An estimated third of the world's population speaks it (as a first, second, or foreign language). This wasn't always the case. Latin occupied this position when the Roman empire was at the height of its power. The English language (a member of the West Germanic group of languages) almost died during the Norman Conquest of Britain in the eleventh century, when French was spoken at the English court. As a result, a great number of words used in English today come from the French.

Why is English so popular today? Because it is a tool for economic survival. It is not superior to other languages. It just happened to be favored in industry and trade.

There are thousands of languages in the world that are only spoken by a handful of people. This is not unique in history. Languages have come and gone and will continue to do so. The collective body of human existence does not depend on any particular language. Communication is the only thing that matters, and humans will communicate any way they see fit.

The Saviors

Self-appointed saviors of cultures and languages abound. While tribes were holding their all-Indian conference in 1961, "concerned" whites produced their own document: *A White Endorsement of the Right to Be Indian*. The Commission on the Rights, Liberties, and Responsibilities of the American Indian produced a summary report titled *A Program for Indian Citizens*, which said that "No program imposed from above can serve as a substitute for one willed by Indians themselves....An objective which should undergrid all Indian policy is that the Indian individual, the Indian family, and the Indian community be motivated to participate in solving their own problems. The Indian must be given responsibility, must be afforded an opportunity he can utilize, and must develop faith in himself."

Again, the comedy in all this is that these "Indian" objectives were themselves written by non-Indians.

These documents, being from the early 1960s, may seem like ancient history. But they are used to illustrate how long the latest wave of effort to "do something for the Indian" has been going on without any positive result for the tribes of the United States. Assimilation and equal treatment under the law are the only ways American Indians will ever gain the status and position they deserve in America.

It is absurd to even pretend that any one ethnic group can do anything to "preserve" another without obliterating the culture of the one that is being "saved" in the process. But self-righteous intellectuals promote the saving game anyway. In *Man's Rise to Civilization*, Peter Farb mourns everything that is dying in the world: "Primitive cultures are disappearing and at an accelerating pace. The Tasmanians are already gone forever. The Yahgan of Tierra del Fuego, studied by Darwin, are virtually extinct, and every year sees fewer Arunta in Australia and Negritos in the Philippines, fewer Aleuts in Alaska and Ainu in Japan, fewer Bushmen in South Africa and Polynesians in Hawaii....Little is being done to preserve the numerous cultures...To do nothing now is to let our children lament that they never knew the magnificent diversity of mankind because our generation let disappear those who might have taught them."

There is something very disturbing about these pronouncements. They are the words of one intellectual bent on forcing humanity to fit an imagined work of knowledge. They ignore the fact that the rules are set by what we call progress—not by scholars. People in small rural villages in Africa don't want to be "preserved," like pickles in brine. They want electricity, television sets, automobiles. They want to live "like you live in America."

Furthermore, there *are* people writing about dying cultures for posterity. Lewis Mehl-Madrona's book on the differences of modern medicine and Native American healing practices is just one of them. But no one can force the world to read these books, or to practice what they offer.

In the next 200 years, many cultures, including a large part of the one most of us are living today, will be gone, replaced by something else. This is the reality that many of the activists involved in "preserving" cultures need to come to grips with. It's time for them to come down from their moral pedestals and check out the real forces that shape civilizations.

Speculation

It is impossible to show what life would be like for the average American Indian today if one hundred years ago, say, all tribes had been allowed to take full possession of their enclaves and turn them into fully independent nations, landlocked islands in the solid sea of U.S. territory, the way Lesotho is surrounded by South Africa.

Those who still promote secession assume that life for tribal members would be better than it is now if such independent nations had been formed then. Perhaps. But speculation is no substitute for reality. Full assimilation will eventually happen because it won't be possible to survive otherwise in a world where technology and global trade have become the dominant culture.

Law of The Land

With Chief Justice Rehnquist's constitutionally mandated participation in the Senate impeachment trial of President Clinton, there was a possibility that Supreme Court cases might suffer some delay. But the decision on the Mille Lacs case was announced around the time it had been expected—the end of March of 1999—and it was completely lost in the more attention-grabbing news from Kosovo: the beginning of NATO's bombing campaign on Serb targets.

The Supreme Court's decision was a painful setback to supporters of equal treatment under the law for all citizens:

"The Chippewa retain the usufructuary rights guaranteed to them by the 1837 Treaty," said the 24 March 1999 opinion. A majority of five—justices O'Connor, Stevens, Souter, Ginsburg, and Breyer—had agreed. Chief Justice Rehnquist, as well as justices Scalia, Thomas, and Kennedy had dissented.

The decision addressed the three principal arguments set forth in the briefs, even though only two of them had been considered in the oral argument.

1) The 1850 Executive Order by President Taylor used very clear language:

"The privileges granted temporarily to the Chippewa Indians of Mississippi by the Fifth Article of the Treaty made with them on the 29th of July 1837, 'of hunting, fishing and gathering the wild rice, upon the lands, the rivers and the lakes included in the territory ceded' by that treaty to the United States...are hereby revoked; and all of the said Indians remaining on the lands ceded as aforesaid, are required to remove to their unceded lands."

The Court's Majority dismissed President Taylor's words by saying that his 1850 Order was a "Removal Order" that had not been authorized under the Removal Act of 1830, which gave a president the power to give lands west of the Mississippi to tribes willing to exchange lands east of the river for them, as long as the tribes consented. "Because the Chippewa had not consented to removal,..." the Majority opinion reads, "the Removal Act could not provide authority for the President's 1850 removal order."

While it is true that the Removal Act was not applicable to the 1850 Order, the assertion that the Order was a removal order is, just by reading its plain text, clearly forced. In his dissent, Chief Justice Rehnquist wrote: "The structure of the Executive Order is not that of a removal order, with the revocation of the hunting privileges added merely as an afterthought. Instead, the first part of the order (not to mention the bulk of its text) deals with the extinguishment of the Indians' privilege to enter onto the lands ceded to the United States and hunt. Only then (and then only in its final five words) does the Executive Order require the Indians to 'remove to their unceded lands.'"

You Be The Judge

You are a teenager on summer vacation, getting up at eleven every morning. One July day, when you get up, there is a note from your mother on the kitchen counter:

"Your father and I have been discussing the fact that you would benefit from getting a job during what's left of the summer. We have had several unexpected expenses lately and could use a third income at home. I have left next to this note the classifieds section of today's paper and have circled several jobs that we think are suitable for you. Get busy with these job leads as soon as possible; and please wash your dishes after lunch."

Can this be called an Order to Wash the Dishes? Do you tell your parents, two months later, that you didn't bother to get a job because their "order to wash the dishes was out of line"?

Justices O'Connor, Stevens, Souter, Ginsburg, and Breyer were not persuaded that the 1850 Executive Order was anything other than a removal order. Nearly 150 years after President Taylor issued the Order, the five Supreme Court justices in the majority say: "[We] think it is clear that President Taylor intended the 1850 order to stand or fall as a whole. The 1850 order embodied a single, coherent policy, the predominant purpose of which was removal of the Chippewa from the lands that they had ceded to the United States...."

That "we think" shows how much these five justices have gone out of their way to adhere to what Chief Justice Rehnquist called their "upside-down reading of the Executive Order's plain text."

Even if the 1850 Executive Order had been a Removal Order and not applicable under the Removal Act of 1830, article V of the 1837 Treaty itself authorized the revocation portion of President Taylor's Order: "The privilege of hunting, fishing, and gathering the wild rice, upon the lands, the rivers and the lakes included in the territory ceded, is guarantied to the Indians, during the pleasure of the President of the United States."

The five Majority justices did not accept this argument, either. They insisted that "The President's power to issue an Executive

Order must stem either from an Act of Congress or from the Constitution itself."

This is again a contradiction of the facts. The 1837 Treaty *did* stem from an Act of Congress and the Constitution. As per the Treaty Clause in the U.S. Constitution (Article II, Sec. 2), "[The President] shall have the Power, by and with the Advice and Consent of the Senate, to make Treaties, provided two thirds of the Senators present concur."

The 1837 Treaty had been ratified by the Senate, which had made it the supreme law of the land by its Advice and Consent. By ratifying it, the Senate had legitimized every word contained in the Treaty, and Article V of the Treaty clearly states that the President has the authority to issue an Order to terminate the Chippewa's privileges to hunt, fish and gather on the ceded territory. "Treaties, every bit as much as statutes, are sources of law and may also authorize Executive actions," wrote Chief Justice Rehnquist in his dissent.

Nevertheless, the Supreme Court's Majority Decision: "[T]he proposition that the 1837 Treaty authorized the President's 1850 removal order is unfounded."

2) The language in the 1855 Treaty is equally simple:

"And the said Indians do further fully and entirely relinquish and convey to the United States, any and all right, title, and interest, of whatsoever nature the same may be, which they may now have in, and to any other lands in the Territory of Minnesota or elsewhere."

The Supreme Court's Majority Decision: "This sentence, however, does not mention the 1837 Treaty, and it does not mention hunting, fishing, and gathering rights." Therefore: "The Mille Lacs Band did not relinquish its 1837 Treaty rights in the 1855 Treaty."

From now on, as per the Supreme Court's decision in the Mille Lacs case, "any and all right, title, and interest, of whatsoever nature" no longer means "any and all right, title, and interest, of whatsoever nature." This is because, according to the Majority opinion, treaties must be interpreted not by their clear language but by "how the Chippewa signatories to the Treaty understood the agreement....The Treaty must be interpreted in light of the parties' intentions, with any ambiguities resolved in favor of the Indians."

3) The Act of 11 May 1858, which made Minnesota a state of the Union, is also written with the same, clear language of the 1850 Order and the 1855 Treaty:

"[T]he State of Minnesota shall be one, and is hereby declared to be one, of the United States of America, and admitted into the Union on an equal footing with the original States *in all respects whatever*." [Emphasis added.]

The Supreme Court's Majority Decision—in what dissenting Chief Justice Rehnquist called a feat of jurisprudential legerdemain—said, "This language, like the rest of the Act, makes no mention of Indian treaty rights." Therefore: "The Chippewa's usufructuary rights were not extinguished when Minnesota was admitted to the Union. Congress must clearly express an intent to abrogate Indian treaty rights....statehood by itself is insufficient to extinguish such rights....There is no suggestion in the 1837 Treaty that the Senate intended the [usufructuary] rights here to terminate when a State was established in the area."

Usufruct. In the civil law, a real right *of **limited duration*** on the property of another. (Emphasis added.)

Usufructuary. In the civil law, one who has the usufruct or right of enjoying anything in which he has no property.

— Black's Law Dictionary (6th ed. 1990)

In summary, justices O'Connor, Stevens, Souter, Ginsburg, and Breyer, a majority of one in the Court, refuted all three arguments by saying that the Chippewa's temporary usufructuary rights to fish, hunt, and gather still exist more than 160 years after they were granted in the 1837 Treaty. Chief Justice Rehnquist wrote in his dissent: "The Court today invalidates for no principled reason a 149-year-old Executive Order, ignores the plain meaning of a 144-year-old treaty provision, and overrules *sub silentio* a 103-year-old precedent of this Court. I dissent."

And so did Justices Scalia, Thomas, and Kennedy.

Reality Check

The Big Picture

A great deal of background noise is being generated by those who are said to be "pro-Indian." It takes mostly the form of litigation and loud public relations campaigns. The challenge is to see the commotion for what it is—a large, activist movement that is fighting to maintain and increase different treatment under the law for less than one percent of the United States population, and to do it with the aid of sympathetic judges.

As a result of the Supreme Court's 1999 Mille Lacs decision, the activism can now be expected to become increasingly fervent. A few examples of what shape it has taken and may be expected to take in the near future:

- Twin Cities: On Sale

In 1994, the Shakopee Mdewakanton Sioux—whose members each earn $600,000 a year from gambling operations—paid close to $4.5 million for 593 acres on the outskirts of the Minneapolis/St. Paul metropolitan area. After contributing $100,000 to the Democratic Party, the tribe asked the Interior Department to turn the 593 acres into tax-exempt "trust lands" for the benefit of the tribe. This is one way in which the federal government has been taking land away from state jurisdiction: Tribes rich with gambling profits get to expand their reservations by purchasing public land, then requesting that it be turned into "Indian Country" by the Interior Department. Such requests have been "routinely granted," according to an Associated Press report. Once public land is labeled as Indian Country, it can never be sold to non-Indians again without the approval of the Federal government. The land is not subject to local property taxes, zoning laws and environmental regulations.

The same Shakopee Mdewakanton Sioux successfully lobbied Interior Secretary Bruce Babbitt to deny a casino license to a competing tribe in Hudson, Wisconsin. Babbitt denied that the tribe's political contribution had influenced his decision to reject the Hudson license. He cited local opposition to the casino as the reason. But local opposition to turning the 593 Twin Cities acres into tribal land did not seem to affect him the same way.

U.S. Senator Rod Grams wrote at the time that no one was suggesting that the tribe had no right to own or develop the land—as long as it paid the taxes required by the state and county governments and observed local development and zoning laws.

But the Shakopee Mdewakanton Sioux preferred different treatment under the law. They wanted Bruce Babbitt to turn their chunk of the Twin Cities into their own playground, where they could play under their own rules and not have to contribute their share of tax revenue—an estimated $94 million in the twelve-year period to come—like everyone else.

• "We Check ID"

Tribal membership ID cards have become special hunting and fishing licenses for those who hold one. On the Great Lakes, the Michigan Department of Natural Resources instructs its conservation officers to request a tribal ID card upon contacting individuals, then "base enforcement accordingly." This refers to the different treatment given to individuals based on their ethnic background. In Michigan's western Upper Peninsula, says James Ekdahl of the Michigan DNR, "Conservation Officers...have a working knowledge of tribal regulations. Violations of tribal law [by tribal members] on lands or waters open to *public hunting or fishing* are turned over to tribal enforcement folks, and prosecuted in tribal court." [Emphasis added.]

• Liberty Island

Another publicity stunt was launched in late 1998 by Timothy J. Stoddard, a "three-eighths Mohegan," who sued the United States over ownership of the home to the Statue of Liberty. Stoddard wants the International Court of Justice at The Hague, Netherlands, to decide who owns the island. His view is that the land was never transferred to the U.S. by any means and so it still belongs to the tribe. "We want to be seen as a sovereign nation whose land was usurped," he said after filing the suit.

Lace Liebman, a professor of property law at Columbia University, indicated that similar suits are being filed in several continents by indigenous peoples who claim title to land once occupied by their ancestors.

• Gambling in Wisconsin

According to the Bureau of Indian Affairs, "State gaming regulations do not apply on Indian trust land." But the Indian Gaming Regulatory Act of 1988 dictates that a "compact" must be signed between the State and a tribe when the gaming involves such things as cards or slot machines. By early

1998, there were some 145 Tribal-State gaming compacts, and Wisconsin had plans to negotiate better terms when its own came up for renewal. Indian Casino operations in the state turned out to be so lucrative—up to $17 billion played a year by mid-1997, yielding revenues of $425 million—that Governor Tommy Thompson felt the State should get a more equitable share of the profits (above the $350,000 it received to cover regulatory costs). Governor Thompson won a victory when one of the eleven tribes with casino operations in the state, the Oneida Nation, later agreed to pay Wisconsin nearly $5 million a year for the right to operate a casino for five additional years, even though surveys showed that a third of the Oneidas insisted they should pay nothing.

• Chicago $ounds Good

Since there is more money to be made running a casino near Chicago than in Kansas, the Potawatomie Prairie Band of Kansas tried to reclaim its "lost homeland" near the Windy City by saying that its ancestral land had been "illegally seized and then sold by the federal government in 1849."

The September, 1998, petition, reported by William Claiborne in the *Washington Post*, was "one of more than a dozen such reclamation efforts from coast to coast, promoted as a way to right the wrongs inflicted on scores of Indian tribes by forced relocations more than a century ago."

The ancestral land in question consists of 1,280 acres sixty miles west of Chicago. The tribe insists that it has no plans to build a casino, but it can certainly change its mind later. "Economic development is the name of the game," said one member.

Claiming ancestral lands near large metropolitan areas where casino profits can be significant has become a trend.

Since passage of the Indian Gaming Regulatory Act of 1988, Indian gaming has prospered. Where bingo halls once provided a modest income, casinos rise to make the owner tribes fantastically wealthy. Hence, the Delaware Indians of western Oklahoma have their eyes on thousands of acres in and around Wildwood, New Jersey—the ancestral homeland from which they were pushed out in the 1830s.

• Texas, too...and New Mexico, and...

Voters in Texas approved a state lottery but not casino gambling. Nevertheless, the Tigua Indian Reservation set up an illegal gaming operation on the southeast side of El Paso.

In New Mexico, the Mescalero Apache refused to sign a casino compact with the state because they didn't want to pay the 16% tax the state was demanding. The tribe considers itself a federal government entity. As such, its members are not subject to any form of state taxation. "We refuse to pay," said Wendell Chino, the tribe's chairman.

This sovereign-government-entity mentality gives Native sovereignty nationalists the right to think of reservations as equal to, and separate from, the established fifty states. Since California cannot levy taxes on Arizona, their reasoning goes, why should Arizona be allowed to touch the self-ruling status of any reservation inside its borders?

As far as every American citizen knows, there is only one State of Arizona, and the shape of the land it occupies is clear on any U.S. map.

Arizona
As We Know It

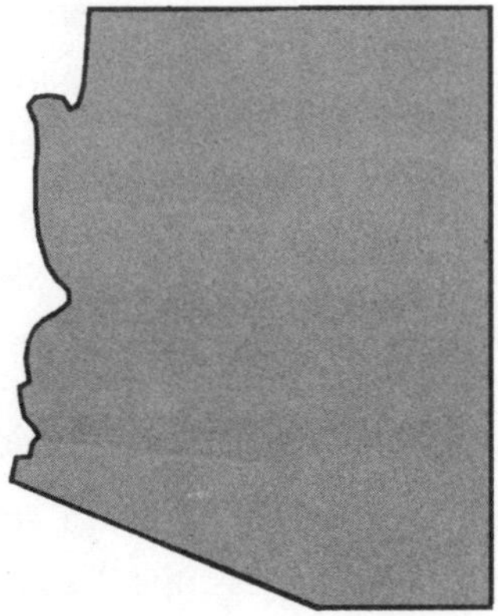

There are no pockets of "Independent, Sovereign Nations" on this map, no Arizonan Lesothos. But Native sovereignty nationalists would like the Grand Canyon State to look like this:

Arizona
The Sovereignty Nationalists' Version

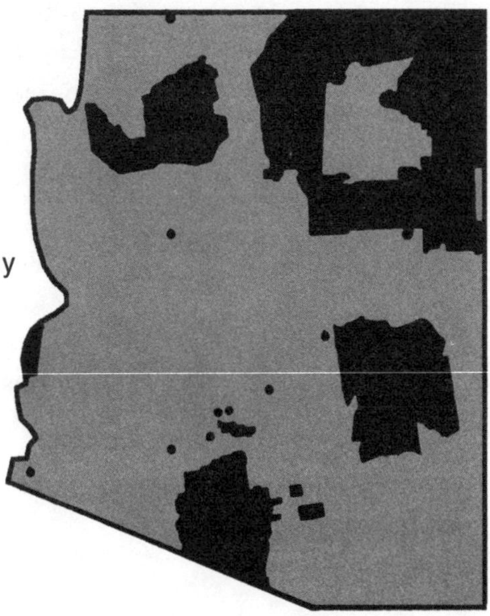

To establish such a divided version of Arizona, under our current political system, a legislative process must be put in motion and be supported by all American voters first.

• The Kings of King County

Kings don't have to follow the same rules as the masses. Neither do the Muckleshoot Indians of King County, Washington. In mid-1998, their building of a $30 million, 23,000-seat amphitheater was in full swing. It was being constructed in violation of local land-use codes, in an area designated as agricultural and rural by the county's comprehensive development plan. The Muckleshoots claimed to be exempt from those laws because of their status as a "sovereign nation," free to ignore the codes and regulations imposed on the community where the amphitheater was being built. The fact that the construction was opposed by neighboring communities didn't count for much. In fact, the citizens of King County had voted to tax themselves to purchase development rights in the area so that it would be reserved "for rural and agricultural uses."

Still, the Kings of King County could do as they pleased. As the British business magazine *The Economist* reported in 1998: "Some Indians…can be brusquely dismissive of those who disagree with them, and the practiced ease with which they play the role of the aggrieved also irritates other Americans. Whether the issue is taxation, gambling or land-use, the tribes tend to argue that the abuse they suffered in the past justifies anything they do now."

In these days of sensitive journalism, no American publication of national scope and distribution could have described this reality with equally biting accuracy.

• Reverse Colonization

In December of 1998, the Oneida tribe of New York, along with the U.S. Department of Justice and other Oneidas from Wisconsin and Ontario, Canada, decided to amend an earlier complaint they had filed against Madison and Oneida counties in the State of New York.

The original lawsuit alleged that land had been illegally transferred from the tribe through various treaties dating back 200 years. The treaties were invalid and violated federal law, the lawsuit claimed. The amendment sought to expand the amount of land in question to more than 250,000 acres (approximately 65% of Madison County and 25% of Oneida County). Some 20,000 individual property owners, most of them non-Indian, live in the affected area. The federal government seeks to help the Oneida establish "sovereign control" over the fee-simple, private property of 20,000 American citizens living in the United States of America.

And it won't stop there. "In the pantheon of Indian law," writes Stacy A. Teicher in *The Christian Science Monitor*, "this case paved the way for at least a half dozen Indian land claims on the East Coast, stretching from Maine to South Carolina."

• Dismantling The U.S.A.

Native nationalism is not limited to the continental United States. The "Hawaiian Kingdom" held a press conference in the summer of 1998 to announce the filing of a complaint in the U.S. Supreme Court, demanding compliance with the "Treaty and Conventions of 1849, 1875 and 1884 between the Hawaiian Kingdom and the United States of America."

The complaint was filed by David Keanu Sai, "Regent, pro tempore," of the Hawaiian Kingdom, which sought, among other things…

- "That a decree be entered ordering [the U.S.A.] to pay reparations for…violations of the 1849 Treaty of Friendship, Commerce and Navigation; the 1875 Commercial Reciprocity Convention; the 1884 Supplementary Convention; the 1993 Apology Law, and principles of customary international law related to the Hawaiian Kingdom and its Subjects, the Native Hawaiian People…;" and
- "That a decree be entered ordering *restitution in integrum* for the Hawaiian Kingdom…[and] for such other and further relief that this Court may deem proper and necessary." [Emphasis added.]

International Law professor Francis Anthony Boyle, of the University of Illinois School of Law, had this to say about the occasion:

> I stand in proud support of David Keanu Sai and this historically important lawsuit that he and the Office of the Regent of the Hawaiian Kingdom are starting against the United States government in order to restore the Hawaiian Kingdom. One hundred five years ago, the Hawaiian Kingdom was stolen by a group of American citizens acting with the illegal support of the United States government. Thieves cannot obtain or convey valid title to anything. As this lawsuit will establish, the United States never lawfully acquired the Hawaiian Kingdom. Despite 105 years of aggression, colonialism, military occupation, and genocide, the Hawaiian Kingdom still exists. It is up to each and every one of us to do whatever we can in our own way and in accordance with our own talents to restore the Hawaiian Kingdom as an Independent Nation State, and with full-fledged Membership in the United Nations Organization.

The filing was followed by an "Aloha March" and two days of planned demonstrations that the organizers hoped would focus national attention on their demands.

Chief Billy Red Wing Tayac, of the Piscataway Indian tribe in Washington State, was there to lend a hand. "We're the same people," he said. "Our land also was stolen. We support the Hawaiian people 125 percent and we hope their land someday will be returned to them."

The American public may dismiss this as inconsequential to the stability of the country, as being "just a bunch of Hawaiians" doing the quintessentially American thing: demonstrating. But national-sovereignty movements are not a joke. There are vast economic interests underlying them that make it worth it for the potential beneficiaries to spend great amounts of money in litigation and lobbying in order to get their way, while undermining the U.S. Constitution and the stability of the country.

• AIM Activism

The American Indian Movement (AIM) is not what it used to be in the 1960s and '70s, when Hollywood (Marlon Brando) and highly visible demonstrations (Alcatraz, the taking of BIA headquarters, and Wounded Knee) kept them in the limelight.

Publicity stunts can only work for so long, though. The public gets tired of them, and AIM is not nearly as influential today as are some of the tribes growing wealthy with casino profits.

Nevertheless, AIM activism goes on in the background, most of it kept out of sight by the publication of distracting, harmless rants on the Internet and alternative media. In California, where the potential for Indian gaming is huge, tribes have been purchasing land and trying to turn it into Indian Country. Because that hasn't been easy, the California AIM chapter brings out its Genocide banner and accuses the state of choosing "to carry into the millennium a policy that was started over a century ago, a policy of abolition for the Native peoples of California," and of consistently opposing "tribes in nearly every aspect of life, liberty and the pursuit of happiness." AIM does not mention the $60 million that tribes spent on the campaign to approve plans for expanding casino gambling in California.

In issue #39 of the journal *Anarchy*, Jason McQuinn reviews *Struggle for the Land: Indigenous Resistance to Genocide, Ecocide and Expropriation in Contemporary North America*, by Ward Churchill, a well known AIM activist. In 472 pages, Churchill offers chapters that examine the "doctrine of U.S. rights to occupancy in North America," "radioactive colonization," and "hydrological rape" of native peoples.

The best part of the book, however, is where Churchill discusses the *Buffalo Commons Project*. That is, "the idea that parts of the Dakotas, Montana, Wyoming, Nebraska, Colorado, Kansas, New Mexico, Oklahoma, Washington state, Idaho, Nevada and Texas, could once again be autonomous Indian territory," writes McQuinn. Churchill's Buffalo Commons Project idea was reprinted in a more recent book of his, *From A Native Son: Selected Essays on Indigenism, 1985-1995*.

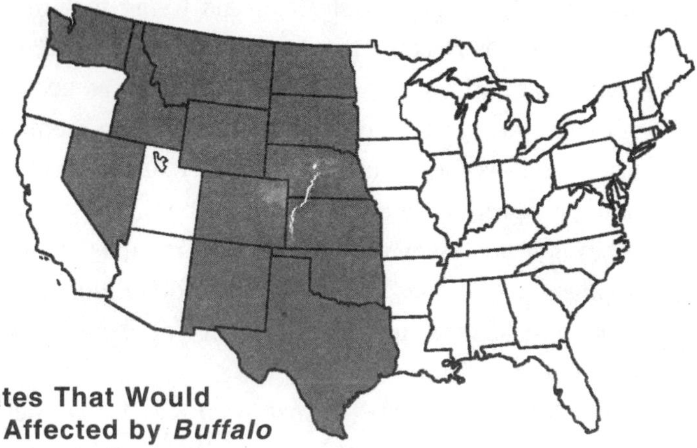

States That Would Be Affected by *Buffalo Commons* Project

The Project is so extreme that most Americans who hear about it are merely amused by it. And that is exactly the goal. Wild land claims such as this one are a diversion tactic. The real activism is going on quietly in the background, through the courts and the gradual but constant undermining of the idea that all citizens should be treated equally under the law.

• Recasting History

In mid-1998, an Indian museum boom was reported. With more than 150 existing Indian museums, and dozens more in the planning stages, the construction of a $193 million "monument to Indian pride and casino prosperity" in rural Connecticut marked a turning point. Now tribes would finally be able to "rewrite their own pages of history," reported Michael Stoll in *The Christian Science Monitor*.

Indian museums are not only tourist destinations or establishments for enlightening the world about what really happened in the Americas after Columbus, according to the tribes. The museums are also seen as community centers where members of a tribe can receive language instruction and hold meetings. Some museums "include exhibits of spiritually significant items for Indian eyes only," wrote Stoll. What museum in the U.S. could get away with an exhibit "for White eyes only"?

• Conflict of Interest

A January 1997 headline stated: "Tribe Battles Park Service To Build in Everglades."

Less than a year earlier, Vice President Al Gore had announced a $1.5 billion "new plan" to restore the Everglades' fragile eco-system to its former glory. "We bear responsibility to protect the world we live in," he said, and blamed farming and development for destroying the Florida wetlands.

"What we are announcing is more than a restoration plan," Gore added. "It is in its purest sense an investment in Florida's future and an investment in America's future." The new plan included the acquisition of 126,000 acres that were being used mostly for sugar farming at the time.

The Miccosukee Indians had already decided to further develop their reservation on the northern edge of the Everglades by building sixty-five new houses. When the park service tried to block construction of the last thirty-five houses due to environmental concerns, the tribe sued, saying it did not need anybody's approval to build on its property.

As a group of Florida congressmen put together a bill declaring that the tribe had "the authority to build what it wants, where it wants on its reservation," the case was being closely followed by other tribes in similar circumstances across the country, where development projects were also at odds with Native Americans' role as "true stewards" of the ecosystem.

In addition, new housing was key to the Miccosukees' cultural survival, the tribe said. "When you lack housing and people are more spread out," said Dexter Lehtinen, the attorney representing the Miccosukees, "[it] has a devastating effect on the culture, on the ability to interact, to speak with each other, to continue the language…the tribal traditions."

Despite his love of nature, Vice President Gore wrote on 21 April 1998, that he was still "committed to the policy of [Indian] self-determination." And that his policy was "to strengthen tribal governments" and "build stable, diversified economies in tribal communities."

Thus, he was still committed to applying laws—even environmental laws—differently on the basis of race.

• Brainwashing: Accomplished?

The notion that reservations are not under American jurisdiction has begun to enter the mainstream. In a recent news release, CDS Signs—a company specializing in the design, manufacture and distribution of "innovative, technology-driven products for the gaming industry"—announced the posting of a new executive to focus on development of "new business in the United States and Canada, as well as Native American jurisdictions."

For a company interested in doing business with Indian casinos, it wouldn't do to offend Native sovereignty nationalists by just saying "business in the United States and Canada." Yet, adding "Native American jurisdictions" to the sentence is as incongruous as adding "Texas" to it.

• Canada, too

Canada now signs treaties with its own citizens. These citizens are not the so-called French-Canadians, who have campaigned for independence from Canada ever since the separatist *Parti Québécois* first won a large majority in the provincial assembly in 1976. No, the privileged people signing a treaty with Canada in 1998 were the Nisga'a Indians of British Columbia, whose nearly 6,000 members stood to receive 745 square miles of land, plus extensive self-government rights, and $320 million.

The treaty was the first on land claims this century. But since there are some fifty other Native groups in British Columbia eager to sign similar treaties, the whole of the province could eventually end up under the legal, social, and economic control of these favored groups.

This is what Native sovereignty nationalists dream of in the U.S.—to go back to treaty-signing at the end of the twentieth century.

In November of 1998, British Columbia lawmakers heard arguments on the Nisga'a Treaty in preparation for a vote. As of June 1999, the Canadian Parliament had not ratified the treaty. Opponents argued that such a treaty could not be ratified without amending the Canadian Constitution.

In the early 1990s, another Canadian native group, the Inuit, signed an agreement for the transfer of roughly one-fifth the land mass of Canada (an area as large as Western Europe) to Inuit control. The area has a population of only 25,000 people, and the agreement called for cash payments of $1.4 billion to the Inuit, paid over a fourteen-year period. This new territory was put on the map as *Nunavut*, the Inuit word for "our home," in April of 1999. Nunavut's premier is Paul Okalik, a 34-year-old lawyer with no previous political experience.

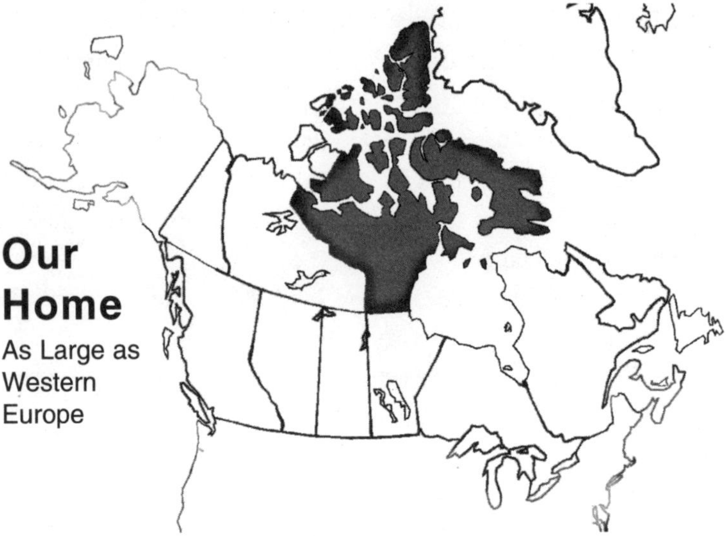

Our Home
As Large as Western Europe

The Inuit will try to keep Nunavut theirs by passing laws that exclude outsiders, like a five-year residency requirement described in *The Native Americans: An Illustrated History* as a measure to "ensure Nunavut stays a native political entity," while the *Miami Herald* reported that "Nunavut will rely on [Canadian] federal funds for 90 percent of its budget."

- Sovereign Immunity

An analysis by the Library of Congress has determined that sovereign immunity is not guaranteed to tribes in any Indian treaty, federal statute, or the U.S. Constitution.

Yet, tribes have become more and more determined on the issue of sovereignty rights. The battle cry of "Sovereign Immunity" is a staple in nearly every lawsuit involving Indian tribes in the United States today. It derives from the idea that tribes have sovereignty.

What is sovereignty? Black's Law Dictionary defines it as follows: "The supreme, absolute, and uncontrollable power by which any independent state is governed; supreme political authority; the supreme will; paramount control of the constitution and frame of government and its administration; the self-sufficient source of political power, from which all specific political powers are derived; the international independence of a state, combined with the right and power of regulating its internal affairs without foreign dictation; also a political society, or state, which is sovereign and independent."

Based on this definition, the idea that tribes have sovereignty is a fantasy. It is obvious that the word means different things to different people.

When title to land that had been erroneously taken by the government was restored to the Red Lake Chippewa, Roger Jourdain, the tribe's Chairman at the time, said, "This land was the aboriginal land of the Red Lake Chippewa...We have sovereign control of it."

What exactly did he mean by this last sentence? It was not Black's Law's definition of sovereign control.

Once a tribe is considered to have sovereignty, it also acquires sovereign immunity. This is appealing because it means the tribe cannot be sued in any U.S. Court. It has immunity. Derril Jordan, the associate solicitor of Indian affairs in the Department of Interior, is very keen on immunity. He is afraid tribes may be exposed to financial losses if they are sued. "Without sovereign immunity," he told the Senate Committee on Indian Affairs in 1998, "the assets of many tribal governments would soon be depleted to the point where meaningful self-government would be untenable."

One might ask: If a local government—a tribal government—cannot take responsibility for its actions in cases of negligence, if it is "untenable" when it has to take that responsibility, then why should it survive as a form of government?

What American citizen would accept a declaration of "sovereign immunity" from a local government as a defense against lawsuits?

Chris Vance, Vice Chairman of the Metropolitan Council of King County, Washington, told the same Senate Committee hearing that if tribes refuse to respect the rights of their neighbors, "then we should at least have…the right to go to court to protect ourselves and be compensated for damages."

Yet, instead of treating all citizens equally under the law and doing away with all the useless litigation, Congress continues to introduce legislation that "negotiates" sovereignty. The farce just goes on.

At one time, most tribes refused to pay sales taxes to states by invoking sovereignty and its attendant immunity. When it was obvious that they could not get away with it much longer, several tribes worked out agreements with states to collect and pay sales taxes—while retaining sovereignty. Impossible. A nation cannot agree to pay taxes to what it considers a foreign nation and still preserve its sovereignty. It is a sham, an insult not only to the U.S. Constitution but to every American Indian.

It is this so-called sovereign immunity that keeps reservation Indians from enjoying the benefit of the Bill of Rights, which applies to all other Americans. Many people are surprised to learn that the Bill of Rights does not apply on reservations. It does not apply because, as Scott Baldauf points out in *The Christian Science Monitor*, "Anglo culture tends to emphasize individual rights, property rights, and total victory, summed up neatly in a Bill of Rights. Indian laws spring from a culture that values harmony and cooperation over the desires of the individual." Baldauf gathered this from a conversation he had with tribal Judge Melvin Stoof, a Rosebud Sioux from South Dakota.

Harmony and cooperation are wonderful ideals, but they can't take place in an atmosphere of racial favoritism. Federal Indian Policy is allowed to go on giving mock sovereignty to Indian tribes because Congress (i.e., the American people) does not have the legislative guts to tell Native sovereignty nationalists, once and for all, that they cannot be American citizens and a sovereign nation at the same time, not under our current Constitution.

• Exempt

The Endangered Species Act (ESA) has been the bane of many a worker in the resource-harvesting industry. In the case of salmon, commercial and sport fisheries have been severely affected by ESA's listing of Chinook Salmon in Puget Sound, Washington.

Yet, it seems that in this case, ESA applies only to non-Indians. Puget Sound and Columbia River Tribes decided not to participate by getting a Secretarial Order (signed by Bruce Babbitt) and an Executive Order (Clinton) allowing them to apply for waivers of ESA restrictions on the fishing of Chinook Salmon.

President Clinton's Executive Order (number 13084, dated 14 May 1998) informs us that tribes "exercise inherent sovereign powers over their members and territory. The United States continues to work with Indian tribes on a government-to-government basis to address issues concerning Indian tribal self-government, trust resources, and Indian tribal treaty and other rights."

Chinook Salmon is a "trust resource."

The order continues: "...to reduce the imposition of unfunded mandates upon Indian tribal governments; and to streamline the application process for and increase the availability of waivers to Indian tribal governments; it is hereby ordered as follows...Each agency shall, to the extent practicable and permitted by law, consider any application by an Indian tribal government for a waiver of statutory or regulatory requirements in connection with any program administered by that agency with a general view toward *increasing opportunities for utilizing flexible policy approaches at the Indian tribal level* in cases in which the proposed waiver is consistent with the applicable Federal policy objectives and is otherwise appropriate." [Emphasis added.]

Once again, racial preference wins the day.

• More Laws, Bad Idea

One proposed solution to race-based laws is the passage of federal legislation in the form of a Tribal Environmental Accountability Act. But such legislation is completely ineffective. It avoids dealing with the real issue—the undermining of the Fourteenth Amendment.

Senator Slade Gorton of Washington State has been the most visible legislator calling for an end to tribal sovereign immunity. In fact, Gorton has gone overboard, introducing all of the following "Indian" bills:

- The American Indian Equal Justice Act—to hold tribes responsible for their actions.
- The Tribal Environmental Accountability Act—to force tribes to comply with federal environmental laws.
- The Indian Civil Rights Enforcement Act—to allow civil rights disputes in tribal courts to be appealed to a federal court.
- The American Indian Tort Liability Act—to require tribes to carry liability insurance.

- The State Excise Sales and Transaction Enforcement Act—to enforce the collection of state sales taxes on sales to non-Indians on a reservation.
- The American Indian Contract Enforcement Act—to enforce contracts between tribes and non-Indians.

More laws and acts are not the answer. If Senator Gorton really believes that Indian tribes should be "subjected to the same responsibility that others are," as he said once, a torrent of confusing legislation is not the way to do it. More laws create more need for enforcement, more police power, more paperwork, more government intervention, more corruption.

When new laws are not based on sound policy—like Gorton's State Excise Sales and Transaction Enforcement Act—the potential for additional controversy and resentment simply multiplies. The Act, for example, is meant to waive tribal sovereign immunity so that state sales tax collection can be enforced on sales to non-tribal members on reservations. It merely tries to create a solution without fixing the actual cause of the problem—the fact that American Indians don't pay sales taxes on reservations, while everyone else does.

War's Over

President Andrew Jackson is accused of having been ruthless when dealing with American Indians. His view was that the United States had no business signing treaties with tribes since they were not independent nations and had no right to their lands.

The accusation is true, but as a former general, and from a military perspective, Jackson had a point: the arrival of Europeans, and their subsequent efforts to populate the American continent, turned out to be a prolonged act of war. Jackson knew this and called it by its name. Few others bothered to do so.

The term "our land was stolen" seems utterly out of context in the history of the United States. The land was not stolen. It was taken. There is a big difference between conquest and theft. During the European invasion, Indian tribes defended themselves bravely. They fought back, endured, and eventually lost. In 1832, Chief Black Hawk acknowledged as much when he surrendered:

"The changes of fortune and vicissitudes of war made you my conqueror," he said. "When my last resources were exhausted, my warriors—worn down with long and toilsome marches—yielded, and I became your prisoner...I am now an obscure member of a nation that formerly honored and respected my opinions. The pathway to glory is rough, and many gloomy hours obscure it. May the Great Spirit shed light on yours, and that you may never experience the humiliation that the power of the American government has reduced me to, is the wish of him who, in his native forests, was once as proud as you."

The conflict between Europeans and Natives was a war from the start. In one case in 1675, three Indians were hanged for allegedly murdering a Christian Indian who had been an informer. Within days of the hangings, fifty-two English towns were attacked in retaliation, twelve completely destroyed. The fighting went on for a year.

More evidence of war:

- Before the French and Indian War, every colony except Pennsylvania and Georgia suffered from bloody warfare.
- The Dutch fought the Algonquian of the Hudson valley and Long Island.
- Maryland colonists were fighting Indians by 1642.
- North Carolina overwhelmed the Tuscarora in 1712.
- South Carolina devastated the Yamassee in 1716.

Constant war. So much so, that those making the profits from the invasion began to worry about business being hurt by so much fighting. That worry led to a Royal Edict in October of 1763—a big mistake for England. The edict forbade colonial settlement west of where the rivers that reached the Atlantic had their sources. But many Europeans had either already settled beyond those points or had their eyes on them, and they refused to obey the King's orders.

His Majesty was then forced to send an army to enforce his rule, and the army was expensive to maintain, so taxes were levied on the colonies to support it. And since that type of abuse of power was exactly what the adventurous frontiersmen had tried to leave behind—in England—soon there was enough opposition to the Royal abuse to fuel what led to Lexington and Concord, the opening battles of the Revolutionary War, on 19 April 1775.

Is the war for the occupation of the American territory still going on? If it is—and the legal battles taking place can certainly be construed as a form of warfare—then it is time to call an end to it. American citizens cannot go on fighting their equals forever. Our Armistice Day can be as close as the day when we decide to stop mocking the Fourteenth Amendment to the U.S. Constitution.

What Next

Dismantle the Bureau

One honest, fair reparation that can be made to Native Americans is to dismantle the phony structure that has been established to "manage" Indian affairs. While the current generation of Americans is not responsible for what happened to American Indians in the past, it certainly has the responsibility to stop the farce that is the BIA.

From almost the beginning, the Bureau assumed the identity of a cozy little factory of corruption. "An Indian Department was made," the Chief of the Oglala Sioux, Red Cloud, said in the 1890s, "with a large number of agents and other officials drawing large salaries....Then came nothing but trouble. These men took care of themselves and not of us." In the wake of the Civil War, agents in the Bureau often worked with corrupt members of Congress to embezzle hundreds of thousands of dollars through a variety of schemes.

Given the ongoing scandal about missing tribal funds, it seems conditions have not changed much, other than the racial composition of the staff: nearly ninety percent of the Bureau's employees are now Native American.

The U.S. Constitution does not have provisions for maintaining Indian "wardship," U.S. government "trust responsibility," or the tribes' status of "domestic dependent nations." The BIA has no reason to exist. It was first created to deal with the war against Indians. Then it turned into a den mother to deal patronizingly with a small group of American citizens who needed to take care of themselves. Finally, it remains today only to deal with white guilt.

Since so many of the transactions with the tribes throughout the history of the United States were acts of hypocrisy, it seems unthinkable to go on with the same bureaucratic-, BIA-approach to things. The United States has a Constitution that opposes the notion of different treatment of citizens through racially specialized bureaus. We must stop apologizing for having such a Constitution, and do away with the BIA.

"Who *is* the United States?" Native sovereignty nationalists may ask. "Who asked for *your* Constitution?" Everybody. Our current system of government is now *in place*. It's what we have. Reality. Chief Justice John Marshall put it best when he said, "However extravagant the pretensions of converting the discovery of an inhabited country into conquest may appear; if the principle has been asserted in the first instance, and afterwards sustained; if a country has been acquired and held under it; if the property of the great mass of the community originates in it, it becomes the law of the land, and cannot be questioned.... However this restriction may be opposed to natural right, and to the usages of civilized nations, yet, if it be indispensable to that system under which the country has been settled, and be adapted to the actual condition of the two people, it may, perhaps, be supported by reason, and certainly cannot be rejected by courts of justice."

Treaties

Abrogate treaties that go counter to the principle of equal treatment under the law for all citizens.

Even in the Supreme Court decision of the Mille Lacs case, the five justices in the Majority stated that, with their decision, they did not mean to "suggest that a President, now or in the future, cannot revoke the Chippewa usufructuary rights in accordance with the terms of the 1837 Treaty. All we conclude today is that the President's 1850 Executive Order was insufficient to accomplish this revocation..."

A simple act of Congress is enough to put an end to all the litigation taking place in the country regarding Indian treaties. Different treatment under the law for a small group of citizens based on treaties is over a hundred years obsolete.

End "Sovereignty"

What entrepreneur or industry will ever dare place a business or factory on a reservation when there are no clear legal guarantees that such effort will be dealt with fairly in case of a lawsuit? Multinational corporations take risks when they invest in certain countries abroad. If the U.S. government allowed American companies to make investments in Cuba, such companies would be exposed to much more risk than, say, investing in Costa Rica.

But when we talk about doing business *inside* the U.S., is it acceptable that Indian reservations are as risky an investment as Cuba? We owe this risk to so-called sovereignty and sovereign immunity. For the well being and economic development of all Indian Americans, the rational path is to abandon the impossible ideal of sovereignty and to join the rest of the country as citizens receiving equal treatment under the law.

Without the farce of sovereignty, reservations become counties in the states where they are located. Tribal courts turn into county courts. One country, one law.

This does not mean that American Indians cannot keep their culture. There are ways in which citizens who share a similar background can establish institutions that maintain their traditions, if they wish to do so. As reservations become counties, and land is distributed among tribal members, individuals can form associations and create large estates that can then be developed for whatever cultural purpose they wish, as long as they follow the same laws everyone else must follow.

In the United States, there has been a rapid growth of gated communities and homeowners' associations in the 1990s. There are some 20,000 private (gated) communities with an estimated four million Americans living in them, and "public" (barricaded) communities with some thirty million. Both pay taxes. Both are subject to state and federal laws. Yet, they offer a sense of the private that approaches that of self-determination.

Ted Turner, better known for his Cable News Network and for donating a billion dollars to the United Nations, owns 1,150,000 acres of land in New Mexico (roughly 1.5 times the size of Rhode Island). As a citizen, and as long as he pays property taxes on the land and adheres to the established regulations, he has the freedom to develop his property to match his vision. Those Native American tribes that have substantial casino profits and earnings can do the same, not as tribes but as individuals or associations of individuals. Ted Turner can get on his horse and get lost in nature in his vast New Mexico estate. If there are still enough Native Americans who want to get lost in nature, they can band together, form a corporation, buy a large estate, and have their private dream. No one would stop them. Their sovereignty would be their privacy.

The goal of ending the nationalist demand for Indian sovereignty in America is also strategic: avoid becoming another Canada (Quebec), Britain (Northern Ireland), Spain (the Basque Country), or Yugoslavia.

Expose

Political posturing must be exposed. Albert Gore's "The President and I support tribal sovereignty" and "We wish to strengthen our government-to-government relationships" must get the intense public scrutiny that the statements deserve. Mr. Gore is simply saying "we support treating you this way if you are Indian, that way if you are not." The well known goal of such a statement is to try to please everyone in order to earn votes. Gore is not the only one doing so, to be sure, and the role of the American public is to expose *all* politicians who engage in this practice.

Political party platforms are incredibly predictable, fill-in-the-blank exercises churned out during every election. Intent on offending the fewest number of voters, they never bother with core beliefs. The thing is to win the election, promising the obviously impossible, even the unconstitutional, without ever saying how it will be achieved.

Political party platforms that promise different treatment under the law to American Indians must be exposed. The promises have been there for years, but no one has ever questioned them—mostly because the politicians, once elected, have totally ignored their promises. Still, that doesn't take away the fact that such "Indian planks" are unconstitutional.

The Republican party was the first to mention Indians in a political platform, in 1872. The Democratic party had its first in 1940. Here is a partial list of the history of empty political promises to American Indians:

- "The treaty and property rights of the Indians of the United States must be guaranteed to them." (Republican, 1928.)
- "We favor…an Indian Claims Commission…in order that

our Indian citizens may have their claims against the Government…finally settled at the earliest possible date." (Democrat, 1940.) [*Finally settled* didn't mean anything since the claims are still going on nearly sixty years later.]

- "We pledge an immediate and final settlement of all Indian claims between the government and the Indian citizenship of the nation." (Republican, 1940.)
- "We pledge an immediate, just and final settlement of all Indian claims between the Government and the Indian citizenship of the Nation. We will take politics out of the administration of Indian affairs." (Republican, 1944.)
- "We demand that Indians, the earliest Americans, be given full citizenship rights without the loss of reservation rights and be permitted to administer their own affairs." (Progressive Henry Wallace, 1948.) [Mr. Wallace's promises are mutually exclusive. It isn't possible to have two sets of rights in a country whose Constitution calls for equal treatment under the law for all citizens.]
- "We shall continue to use the powers of the Federal government to advance the health, education and economic well-being of our American Indian citizens, without impairing their cultural traditions." (Democrat, 1952.) [This qualifies for the Oxymoron Hall of Fame. Cultural traditions are a big part of health and education. But the platform isn't finished:] "The American Indian should be completely integrated into the social, economic and political life of the nation…We favor the repeal of all acts or regulations that deny to Indians rights or privileges held by citizens generally."
- "We shall eliminate the existing shameful waste by the Bureau of Indian Affairs…" (Republican, 1952.)
- "Premature and enforced assimilation of Indians into the

dominant culture is no answer to their special problems." (Socialist, 1960.) [Did this mean that thirty-nine years later assimilation would be expected to be of term?]

- "The plight of American Indians and Eskimos is a national disgrace. [!] Contradictory Government policies have led to intolerable deprivation for these citizens." (Republican, 1968.)
- "We must continue and increase Federal help in the Indian people's battle against poverty, unemployment, illiteracy, ill health and poor housing. To this end, we pledge a new and equal Federal-Indian partnership." (Democrat, 1968.)

The 1996 Democratic National Platform offers pages and pages of Utopian social engineering. In Section IV, under the subtitle *The American Community*, the platform says:

> Today's Democratic Party knows that when America is divided we will likely fail, but when America is united we will always prevail. Americans will always have differences, and when we reach across those differences, we are stronger for it….The Clinton Administration is committed to strengthening the government-to-government relationship between the federal government and the American Indian and Alaska Native tribal governments. The President will continue implementation of the Self-Governance/Self-Determination Act amendments which he signed in 1994 that will eventually open up the self-governance program to all tribal governments who wish to participate, giving these governments full control of where and how certain federal resources are spent on their reservations. We must remember we do not have an American to waste. We continue to lead the fight to end discrimination on the basis of race, gender, religion, age, ethnicity, disability, and sexual orientation….If we do

> our job, we will make the next American century as great as each one that has come before it....America's best days lie ahead, as we renew our historic pledge to uphold and advance the promise of America—One nation, under God, indivisible, with liberty and justice for all.

The Republican Platform for 1996, in a section titled *From Many, One*, has this to offer: "We will strengthen Native Americans' self-determination by respecting tribal sovereignty...We uphold the unique government-to-government relationship between the tribes and the United States."

Even the Libertarian Party plays the game of trying to please everyone with ideological contradictions. Number 8 under their *Individual Rights and Civil Order* category of the platform is "Individual Sovereignty," which states that "the only legitimate use of force is in defense of individual rights...*We favor an immediate end to the doctrine of 'Sovereign Immunity'* which ignores the primacy of the individual over the abstraction of the State, and holds that the State, contrary to the tradition of redress of grievances, may not be sued without its permission or held accountable for its actions under civil law." [Emphasis added.]

Then the platform offers the most startling contradiction, under *American Indian Rights*, Number 23: "Indians should have their property rights restored, including rights of easement, access, hunting, and fishing." Indians, as a *group*, should have their property rights restored. The plank offers no explanation of what this implies. Why is it talking about Indians at all, in the plural, when the supreme being to Libertarians is the individual? Furthermore, as the Mille Lacs 1837 Treaty case has plainly shown, restoring hunting and fishing rights to a favored group tramples on the rights of individual landowners. And don't Libertarians hold private property sacred?

This political posturing must be exposed—relentlessly—more than ever now that, in addition to votes, it seeks political contributions from tribes that have the economic means to demand political payback. The Cheyenne-Arapaho Tribe expected it when it gave the Democratic National Committee (DNC) a $107,000 donation in 1997. The funds had strings attached: the tribe thought it was buying some property, and the DNC later tried to return the donation when it couldn't deliver.

As Indian casino profits increase, making their way to campaign coffers, politicians will not be able to ignore their empty promises anymore. Political platforms will get further away from the idea of equal treatment under the law, and move closer to promising "government-to-government" relationships, sovereignty, and whatever Native sovereignty nationalists demand. These platforms and promises must be exposed for what they are: unconstitutional.

The American People

Don Wedll, the Commissioner of Natural Resources for the Mille Lacs Band of Chippewa, said once that there were no easy answers to the many questions raised by a treaty. "It's best to let the courts work through it," he added.

Both sides of the treaty-rights argument seem to agree. It is easier (and definitely less costly) to let the courts do the work than to participate as citizens.

Others, like Minnesotan Howard Hanson, believe that the issue must be resolved through the legislature and the participation of all Americans. To that end, he founded the Resource Party and ran as its candidate for the U.S. Senate in the 1996 election. One of his goals was to raise public awareness of fishing-rights issues in relation to treaties.

The Resource Party is the only political party (registered in all fifty states) that has a platform addressing the unconstitutionality of Federal Indian Policy. This particular point of the Resource Party's platform deserves attention, but during the 1996 election campaign—as now—it was ignored by the news media. Voters were not informed, other political parties were not forced to address Federal Indian Policy, and Howard Hanson got 4,301 votes (less than one percent).

The prevailing attitude of the news media is that the American public does not want to deal with difficult political issues. Hendrik Hertzberg writes in *The New Yorker*, "Most of the other countries of the democratic world, from Poland to New Zealand—have national political institutions whose representational legitimacy is taken for granted. Most citizens vote in such countries." By contrast, our U.S. House of Representatives "represents" only "about a quarter of the country's eligible voters: that's how many of us voted for one of its four hundred and thirty-five members. (And only about a fifth of that quarter, which is to say around five percent of the total, ever gets to help elect someone in a competitive district, where the result isn't a foregone conclusion.)"

The trick, then, is in getting Americans to participate by knowing the difference between sovereignty and citizenship, and voting their minds in elections. Federal Indian Policy needs to be brought out in the open. A recent survey by the National Constitution Center revealed that 91% of American adults believe the U.S. Constitution is important, and 84% believe that "a successful government relies on an active and informed citizenry." The American public needs to be informed about the legalized racism that is Federal Indian Policy.

Hold Congress Accountable

When Howard Thurber, a Mille Lacs County resident, wrote to Minnesota Senator Paul Wellstone in early 1998 about his concerns regarding the status of the Mille Lacs Indian "Reservation," a reply came not from Senator Wellstone's office but from the Bureau of Indian Affairs, the *least* qualified entity to offer an objective response.

"Your letter was forwarded to this office by United States Senator Paul David Wellstone," wrote Claricy Smith, an Acting Area Director at the Bureau of Indian Affairs. "Our review indicates that the Mille Lacs Indian Reservation continues to exist today as it was described in the Treaty of 1855. There is no indication that the reservation boundaries have ever been diminished since then."

It is very much in the BIA's interest that *all* reservations continue to exist forever.

The Acting Area Director then turned patronizing: "As you may be aware, the parameter of tribal civil authority over non-Indians is an exceeding [sic] complex mater [sic], not subject to generalizations or easy classifications. Nevertheless, our review indicates that an Indian tribe has the inherent right to exercise civil jurisdiction within the territory it controls, including the power to tax." And so on.

Senator Wellstone's non-reply to Thurber's letter is the reason that citizens start relying on the courts for matters that should be taken care of through the Legislative Branch of government, not the Judicial Branch.

In the past few years, federal courts have made rulings on such controversial topics as assisted suicide, abortion, homosexuality, and euthanasia in ways that have created a pattern of government by judges. The courts have appropriated the power to deal with these issues from Congress (i.e., the people) because voters have been unable to deal with them through the legislative process. In doing so, judges have reached "extraconstitutional and illegitimate decisions," writes author Midge Dector to the editors of *First Things*. "It used to be said of the court that its decisions followed election results. But even in these less than attractive times, nothing quite so cynical is the case: what the court actually follows is the *culture*."

The danger in this pattern is that we have grown accustomed to it. We so revere judges and courts and their supposed superior wisdom, that we feel we don't need to participate anymore. As a result, we give validity to what Thomas Sowell calls one of the more remarkable defenses of judicial activism: "that the courts were 'forced' to act because Congress, the president, or other authorities or institutions 'failed' to act."

For this and many other reasons, Federal Indian Policy must be reviewed by Congress and the citizenry, not by courts as "legislatures of last resort." Whatever anthropologists, historians, or linguists may decide, the law of the land must concentrate on serving those living in the present. Public policy must not be dictated by ancestral studies or anthropological grants.

All citizens must get involved in putting an end to our anachronistic Federal Indian Policy, to force political parties to stop promising "sovereignty" and "government-to-government" relationships to a small group of Americans. No winning political party should get its vote based on a plank that divides constituents by race. Promises of special treatment to Native Americans, Blacks, Latinos—or any other minority (or majority)—must end. Political party platforms, from now on, should concentrate on one simple phrase when dealing with the statutory treatment of citizens: One country, one law.

A Voice of Reason

Native sovereignty nationalists are a small minority. They are joined by a few tribal leaders who may not care much for Native nationalism but do have an interest in maintaining the status quo to preserve their positions of power and access to tribal funds.

Both of these groups are greatly outnumbered by the rest of those U.S. citizens who consider themselves American Indians and who cherish their traditions but wish to maintain them with dignity and equal access to American society at large. One of these Americans is Roland Morris, Sr., who offers the following thoughts at an Internet site he and his wife Lisa created to explain why Federal Indian Policy must change:

> "It's time to forgive and move on. No more Blame. We are all adults and fully accountable for our actions. We in the United States have to get past the idea that American Indians must forever be looked at as victims. I, for one, refuse to be viewed that way any longer.
>
> "My name is Roland Morris, Sr. I am a full-blooded Anishinabe American citizen. Originally from the State of Minnesota, I now live in Montana. It is my hope you will discern the truthfulness of my message by examining both my heart, as well as my words.
>
> "When my brothers and sisters and I were growing up in the 50s, the hateful, overt racism did hurt. However, the reverse was also hurtful. When patronizing people essentially pat us on the head and said;

'you poor dear, you are a victim and can't possibly take care of yourself' and 'you can't be to blame for your actions,' that was just as hurtful, if not more so. On top of that, Federal Indian Policy itself views Native Americans as helpless wards.

"With hateful racists on one side putting us down, well meaning liberals on the other side putting us down, and the federal Government there to take care of us anyway, many started to believe what was said about them and succumbed to the expectations of all sides. How should one feel when as a man, one is treated as a child?

"Please understand, Chief Joseph was right when he said, 'we only ask a chance to live as other men live.'

"I ask for nothing 'special.' To receive something 'special' means I will be treated differently and separately from other men.

"Government dependence, through current Federal Indian Policy, is killing people. Federal Policy currently treats tribal members as wards, as children. A man needs to feel needed, but as long as the government is taking care of a man's family through welfare, food stamps, fuel assistance, Medicaid, and HUD housing, a man loses that feeling of being needed and important to his family. If a man doesn't feel needed, what is there for him?

"I have to ask myself, and you as well...are Indian people to be considered separate but more equal, separate but less equal, or separate and equal? And is it necessary to be separate anyway?

"Secondly, Tribal governments have become dependent on Federal government help. Through this dependency, many tribal governments have become corrupt with unchecked power and money. Because of this corruption and unwillingness to let go of power and money, tribal government themselves, in some cases, are keeping their people in the bondage of poverty and oppression. In addition, we have seen tribal governments, in order to keep power and money, attempt to keep outsiders sympathetic by using pictures of poor, disheveled elderly and children. The tribal gambling industry did this in the fall of 1997.

"Isn't this an abuse of the people? I also see true elders feeling defeated. Young people won't listen to how the elders want to handle the situation. Seeing this disrespect is hurtful to me.

"It can be no wonder that Indian people are tired and depressed. Not only do many feel alienated from the United States Government, but many tribal governments can't be trusted either. Through this depression and loss of hope, people are dying of alcoholism, drug abuse, suicide and violence. Some die quickly, others die slowly. Some live years but are dead in their hearts. If the current system is so good for Native people, why is this happening?

"Current Federal Indian Policy is also hurting non-tribal members. Many treaty provisions were meant to last only twenty or so years. It has been Congress and tribal governments that have been stretching it out longer. Now, some tribal governments, again in (an) effort to keep money and control, use guilt and pity to keep American taxpayers from putting an end to the funding. And politicians, either afraid of seeming cold-hearted or because tribal governments make huge campaign contributions, turn and look the other way.

"How do we fix the problem? That is the question. Many elders are distressed at the thought of giving up even more tribal autonomy. Too much has been lost already. These elders need to be respected and listened to. Other elders say we have lost hope and happiness, and without these, what is everything else worth? If the power structure continues as it is now, angering and estranging people, creating a society full of hopelessness, drug abuse, violence, and hate, what good (are) all the assets we have left anyway?

"Is there a way to make the situation more healthy for everyone without giving up tribal assets? Can we work this out so that elders feel they are heard, tribal members get what they need, and non-members aren't trod on?

"With the current epidemic of corruption on Indian Reservations, how could tribal members be better protected? It is clear to us that some kind of discussion needs to begin. We can't continue to sit back and watch relatives die.

"Lastly, pain, rejection and persecution are not factors isolated to one people group. In fact, all people have their own crosses to bear, pain to hide. Christ went to the cross, beaten and spit upon, but blaming no one and without self-pity. If we are to come together as people, we must follow his example of forgiveness.

> "Native Americans are not more 'needy' than anyone else. In fact, Native Americans are just as good and just as evil, just as productive and just as non-productive, as any other people."

Amend

In the early 1970s, Native American scholar Vine Deloria, Jr., made a call similar to the one by Roland Morris, Sr.: "The time has come when it is clearly in the best interest of the United States to clarify the legal status of Indians."

That clarification is due now, at the end of the century. And because so many great minds don't seem to grasp the simple language of the Fourteenth Amendment to the Constitution, American citizens should consider passing another amendment, called the Equal Laws Amendment (ELA), which might read something like this:

Amendment XXVIII

Section 1. All persons born or naturalized in the United States shall be subject to the **same** federal laws **regardless of** race, sex, economic status, religion or any other classification that may arise. All persons born or naturalized in the United States shall be subject to the **same** State laws of the state in which they reside **regardless of** race, sex, economic status, religion or any other classification that may arise. This Amendment supercedes any and all laws, acts, provisions, treaties or legislation previously ratified.

Section 2. The Congress shall have power to enforce this article by appropriate legislation.

The ELA would be a legislative move that would involve all Americans through their representatives in Congress. The alternative, as already mentioned, is to let the courts decide for us and allow the Judicial Branch of government (with its many activist judges) to run the show. The courts were set up to review the law. Sovereignty and treaty rights are clearly cases where the law needs to be changed, not reviewed or misinterpreted by those who believe that treating citizens differently under the law, according to race, is the way to the enduring unity of the United States.

Avoiding the Irish and Roman Paths

The issue of sovereignty and self-determination has been responsible for the deaths of thousands of people and much suffering in the world. Self-determination, writes Fintan O'Toole, is the "most important word in the lexicon of nations. It's what the American colonists wanted in 1776, and it's what the United Nations guarantees its members. But who gets to use it?"

In the case of Ireland—where Irish Protestants wanted the island to belong to the United Kingdom, and Irish Catholics did not—an agreement was worked in 1920 whereby the island was partitioned, with Catholics eventually becoming the independent Republic of Ireland (on about eighty-four percent of the land) and Protestants forming a political division of the United Kingdom, called Northern Ireland (on the rest). As everyone knows, the settlement never satisfied sovereignty nationalists on both sides. Extreme nationalists can never be satisfied.

In addition, the Catholics who had been living in what became Northern Ireland did not want to move south to join their Catholic brothers. So Catholic extremists in Northern Ireland took it upon themselves to speak for all Catholics. They gained notoriety as the Irish Republican Army (IRA), demanding self-determination with gruesome terrorist acts, and achieving nothing but a lot of suffering and pain for both sides.

The United States isn't Ireland, of course. Native Americans are not one people but a collection of ethnic groups (more than 550) with different traditions and interests. In proportion, Native American land claims have affected a relatively small segment of the non-Indian population, and have gone unnoticed as a result. But as more and more lawsuits are filed, and more casino profits are poured into the sovereignty nationalist effort to divide the population along racial lines, our refusal to deal with the issue of Native American sovereignty and self-determination will have severe effects on the long-term social harmony of the country's population, and it may very well lead us down the path of the Irish—and the Romans. To quote historian Thomas Cahill: "What we can say with confidence is that Rome fell gradually and that Romans for many decades scarcely noticed what was happening."

Perhaps we should start noticing.

Appendix

Treaty of July 29, 1837

Articles of a treaty made and concluded at St. Peters [the confluence of the St. Peters and Mississippi rivers] in the Territory of Wisconsin, between the United States of America, by their commissioner, Henry Dodge, Governor of said Territory, and the Chippewa nation of Indians, by their chiefs and headmen.

ARTICLE 1. The said Chippewa nation cede to the United States all the tract of country included within the following boundaries:

Beginning at the junction of the Crow Wing and Mississippi rivers, between twenty and thirty miles above where the Mississippi is crossed by the forty-sixth parallel of north latitude, and running thence to the north point of Lake St. Croix, one of the sources of the St. Croix river; thence to and along the dividing ridge between the waters of Lake Superior and those of the Mississippi, to the sources of the Ocha-sua-sepe a tributary of the Chippewa river; thence to a point on the Chippewa river, twenty miles below the outlet of Lake De Flambeau; thence to the junction of the Wisconsin and Pelican rivers; thence on an east course twenty-five miles;

thence southerly, on a course parallel with that of the Wisconsin river, to the line dividing the territories of the Chippewas and Menominees; thence to the Plover Portage; thence along the southern boundary of the Chippewa country, to the commencement of the boundary line dividing it from that of the Sioux, half a days march below the falls on the Chippewa river; thence with said boundary line to the mouth of Wah-tap river; at its junction with the Mississippi; and thence up the Mississippi to the place of beginning.

ARTICLE 2. In consideration of the cession aforesaid, the United States agrees to make to the Chippewa nation, annually, for the term of twenty years, from the date of the ratification of this treaty, the following payments.

Nine thousand five hundred dollars, to be paid in money.

Nineteen thousand dollars, to be delivered in goods.

Three thousand dollars for establishing three blacksmith shops, supporting the blacksmiths, and furnishing them with iron and steel. One thousand dollars for farmers, and for supplying them and the Indians, with implements of labor, with grain or seed; and whatever else may be necessary to enable them to carry on their agricultural pursuits.

Two thousand dollars in provisions.

Five hundred dollars in tobacco.

The provisions and tobacco to be delivered at the same time with the goods, and the money to be paid; which time or times, as well as the place or places where they are to be delivered, shall be fixed upon under the direction of the President of the United States.

The blacksmiths shops to be placed at such points in the Chippewa country as shall be designated by the Superintendent of Indian Affairs, or under his direction.

If at the expiration of one or more years the Indians should prefer to receive goods, instead of the nine thousand dollars agreed to be paid to them in money, they shall be at liberty to do so. Or, should they conclude to appropriate a portion of that annuity to the establishment and support of a school or schools among them, this shall be granted them.

ARTICLE 3. The sum of one hundred thousand dollars shall be paid by the United States, to the half-breeds of the Chippewa nation, under the direction of the President. It is the wish of the Indians that their two sub-agents Daniel P. Bushnell, and Miles M. Vineyard, superintend the distribution of this money among their half-breed relations.

ARTICLE 4. The sum of seventy thousand dollars shall be applied to the payment, by the United States, of certain claims against the Indians of which amount twenty-eight thousand dollars shall, at their request, be paid to William A. Aitkin, twenty-five thousand to Lyman M. Warren, and the balance applied to the liquidation of other just demands against them — which they acknowledge to be the case with regard to that presented by Hercules L. Dousman, for the sum of five thousand dollars; and they request that it be paid.

ARTICLE 5. The privilege of hunting, fishing, and gathering the wild rice, upon the lands, the rivers and the lakes included in the territory ceded, is guaranteed to the Indians, during the pleasure of the President of the United States.

ARTICLE 6. This treaty shall be obligatory from and after its ratification by the President and Senate of the United States.

Done at St. Peters in the Territory of Wisconsin the twenty-ninth day of July eighteen hundred and thirty-seven.

Henry Dodge, Commissioner

Sources

This book does not pretend to be a scholarly treatise on the fishing, hunting and gathering rights claimed by Native Americans. It is not a legal study of treaty laws or their cultural ramifications. It simply aims to introduce the reader to Federal Indian Policy and its effect on the ideal of equal treatment under the law for all American citizens.

The source material for the book includes newspaper and magazine articles, Internet sites, encyclopedias, history books, activist and political tracts, newsletters, and personal and phone interviews. Old English quotations have been changed to modern English for easier reading.

Like partisan politics, books and articles lean heavily to each of their respective sides of an issue, or they simply omit information. As sources, I intentionally chose a number of popular books that clearly favor Native American sovereignty and different treatment under the law for American Indians. The authors and editors of these books are viewed as supporters of Native Americans. Their writing style leans toward an anti-white racial bias, even when the writers themselves are white. Since the 1960s, it has been the fashion with some intellectuals to curse their own race and generation for what happened in past ages. Their own words are evidence that the worst possible tool to fight racism is racism itself—the reverse form of racism that to them, it seems, is acceptable.

Books

Barsh, Russel Lawrence, and James Y. Henderson. *The Road: Indian Tribes and Political Liberty*. Berkeley: University of California Press, 1982.

Black, Henry Campbell, Joseph R. Nolan (Coauthor), Jacqueline M. Nolan-Haley (Coauthor), Martina N. Alibrandi (Contributor), Stephen C. Hicks (Contributor), and M. J. Connolly (Contributor). *Black's Law Dictionary, 6th Edition*. St. Paul: West Publishing Co., 1991.

Cahill, Thomas. *How the Irish Saved Civilization: The Untold Story of Ireland's Heroic Role from the Fall of Rome to the Rise of Medieval Europe*. New York: Doubleday, 1995.

Canby, William C. *American Indian Law in a Nutshell, 3rd Edition*. St. Paul: West Group, 1998.

Caplan, Lincoln. *The Tenth Justice: The Solicitor General and the Rule of Law*. New York: Alfred A. Knopf, 1987.

Clifton, James A., ed. *The Invented Indian: Cultural Fictions and Government Policies*. Somerset, New Jersey: Transaction, 1994.

Cohen, Felix S. "Americanizing the White Man," *The American Scholar*, Spring, 1952.

Collier, John. *From Every Zenith: A Memoir and Some Essays on Life and Thought*. Denver: Sage Books, 1963.

—. *The Columbia Encyclopedia, 5th Edition.* New York: Columbia University Press, 1993.

—. *Concise Columbia Electronic Encyclopedia* (electronic edition). New York: Columbia University Press, 1994.

Deloria, Jr., Vine. *Behind The Trail of Broken Treaties: An Indian Declaration of Independence*. New York: Dell Publishing Co., Inc., 1974.

de Villiers, Les; Gary Player, and Chris Barnard. *The Travel Guide to South Africa*. New Canaan: Business Books International, 1992.

Farb, Peter. *Man's Rise to Civilization as Shown by the Indians of North America From Primeval Times to The Coming of The Industrial State*. New York: E. P. Dutton & Co., Inc., 1968.

Garrett, Laurie. *The Coming Plague: Newly Emerging Diseases in a World Out of Balance*. New York: Farrar, Straus and Giroux, 1994.

Goulden, Joseph C. *The Benchwarmers: The Private World of the Powerful Federal Judges*. New York: Weybright and Talley, 1974.

Johansen, Bruce Elliott, ed. *The Encyclopedia of Native American Legal Tradition*. Westport, Connecticut: Greenwood Press, 1998.

Josephy, Alvin M., ed., and Frederick E. Hoxie, ed. *America in 1492: The World of the Indian Peoples Before the Arrival of Columbus*. New York: Vintage Books, 1993.

Marks, Paula Mitchell. *In a Barren Land: American Indian Dispossession and Survival*. New York: William Morrow and Company, Inc., 1998.

Mehl-Madrona, Lewis. *Coyote Medicine*. New York: Scribner, 1997.

Mörner, Magnus. *Race Mixture in the History of Latin America*. Boston: Little, Brown, 1967.

—. *The Native Americans: An Illustrated History*. Atlanta: Turner Publishing, Inc., 1993.

Nixon, Richard. "Special Introduction by President Richard Nixon; North Dakota Law Review—Summer 1972," *North Dakota Law Review, Vol. 48, No. 4.*: University of North Dakota School of Law, 1972.

Porter, Kirk Harold, comp. *National Party Platforms, 1840-1956*. Urbana: University of Illinois Press, 1956.

Price, David. *The Second Civil War: Examining the Indian Demand for Ethnic Sovereignty*. St. Paul Park: Second Source, 1998.

Rae, Noel, ed. *Witnessing America: The Library of Congress Book of Firsthand Accounts of Life in America 1600-1900*. New York: Stonesong Press, 1996.

—. *The Reader's Companion to American History* (electronic edition). Boston: Houghton Mifflin, 1991.

Sowell, Thomas. *The Vision of the Anointed: Self-Congratulation as a Basis for Social Policy*. New York: Basic Books, 1995.

Steiner, Stan. *The New Indians*. New York: Harper & Row, 1968.

Tanner, Helen H. *The Settling of North America: The Atlas of the Great Migrations into North America from the Ice Age to the Present*. New York: MacMillan, 1995.

Vazsonyi, Balint. *America's 30 Years War: Who is Winning?* Washington, D.C.: Regnery, 1998.

Vogel, Virgil J. *This Country Was Ours: A Documentary History of The American Indian*. New York: Harper & Row, 1972.

West, Elliot. *The Contested Plains: Indians, Goldseekers and the Rush to Colorado*. Lawrence, KS: University Press of Kansas, 1998.

Winks, Robin W., ed. *The Historian as Detective: Essays on Evidence*. New York: Harper Torchbooks, 1969.

Wright, John W., ed. *The Universal Almanac: A New Almanac for an Expanding Universe of Information*. Kansas City: Universal Press Syndicate, 1996.

Newspapers, Magazines and Newsletters
(print and electronic editions)

- *Anarchy*, issue #39: Winter, 1994. Internet edition, as of November 9, 1998.
- *The Austin Review*: Internet edition, as of January 18, 1999, article dated October 17, 1997.
- *Brainerd Daily Dispatch*: April 20, 1997.
- *The Christian Science Monitor*: November 12, 1996; January 9, 1997; April 3, 1998; June 5, 1998; June 25, 1998; July 7, 1998; August 11, 1998; December 2, 1998; September 8, 1999.

Sources

- *The Chronicle Centralia Washington*: April 13, 1998
- *Civilization*: March/April 1995; October/ November 1996; February/March 1997.
- *Discover magazine*: February 1999.
- *The Drum (Rites of Passage Institute)*: Undated Internet edition, as of May 10, 1999.
- *The Economist*: September 20, 1997; December 19, 1998-January 1, 1999 (double issue).
- *Emerge*: February 1999.
- *The Environmental Magazine*: July-August 1996.
- *Forbes*: November 16, 1998.
- *Forbes ASAP*: August 24, 1998.
- *Granta*: Summer, 1998.
- *Harper's Magazine*: July 1998.
- *Honolulu Star-Bulletin*: August 7, 1998.
- *Indian Country Today*: June 11-18, 1996.
- *International Falls Daily Journal*: September 5, 1997; November 18, 1997; September 2, 1998.
- *Mille Lacs Messenger:* March 6, 1996.
- *Minneapolis Star Tribune*: January 10, 1989; December 15, 1992; December 2, 1994; April 2, 1995; April 8, 1995; October 8, 1995; February 8, 1997; February 10, 1997; February 23, 1997; March 21, 1997; March 28, 1997; June 1, 1997; June 13, 1997; August 27, 1997; August 31, 1997; June 9, 1998; February 21, 1998; February 24, 1998; March 14, 1998; March 20, 1998; April 8, 1998; June 10, 1998; August 5, 1998; December 2, 1998; December 3, 1998.
- *The Minnesota Daily*: February 27, 1998.
- *New York Times*: November 2, 1997; March 8, 1998; November 20, 1998; November 23, 1998; February 23, 1999.
- *The New Yorker*: April 20, 1998; April 27 & May 4, 1998.
- *El Nuevo Herald*: November 17, 1998.

- *Oklahoma Indian Times*: Undated Internet edition, as of November 2, 1998.
- *Outdoor Life*: May 1993.
- *Outdoor News*: April 3, 1992; December 17, 1993; December 24, 1993; October 31, 1997.
- *The Outdoorsman's Weekly*: June 13, 1996.
- *The Resource Sentinel*: January 1995; February 1997.
- *Richmond Times Dispatch*: November 13, 1998.
- *St. Cloud (Minn.) Times*: February 23, 1993.
- *Saint Louis Post-Dispatch*: October 2, 1995.
- *St. Paul Pioneer Press*: May 3, 1992; August 17, 1996.
- *Skagit Valley Herald*: June 8, 1998.
- *Seattle Post-Intelligencer*: May 7, 1998.
- *Spin*: November 1998.
- *Utne Reader*: September-October 1998; January-February 1999; March-April 1999; May–June 1999.
- *Time*: December 7, 1998.
- *Time Daily*: March 27, 1996; March 12, 1997.
- *Washington Inquirer*: May 7, 1993.
- *Washington Post*: January 25, 1998; September 27, 1998; November 1, 1998; December 6, 1998; December 13, 1998; December 15, 1998; December 26, 1998; February 23, 1999.
- *The Wilson Quarterly*: New Year's 1986; Spring 1997; Winter 1997; Winter 1998; Winter 1999.
- *Wisconsin State Journal*: May 9, 1998.

News Wire Services

- *Associated Press*: March 31, 1998; April 2, 1998; April 4, 1998; December 2, 1998; December 3, 1998.
- *Business Wire*: November 20, 1998; November 30, 1998.

- *CNN Environmental News*: February 19, 1996.
- *Reuters*: November 8, 1998; November 17, 1998; November 19, 1998; December 2, 1998; November 30, 1998.
- *States News Service*: “Minnesota Headlines,” December 3, 1998; “Montana Headlines,” December 4, 1998.

Agencies and Government Documents

- Bureau of Indian Affairs letter to Howard Thurber, April 28, 1998.
- Bureau of Indian Affairs' Public Affairs Office's Internet site, as of December 31, 1998.
- Bureau of the Census.
- Fiftieth Congress, Session II, Chapter 24, January 14, 1889.
- U.S. Constitution.
- Department of Defense's *Native American Briefing* report, January 23, 1998.
- Department of the Interior's Internet site. Lands Under the Jurisdiction of the BIA, last updated December 31, 1996.
- Federal Bureau of Labor Statistics, Occupational Outlook Handbook. www.bls.gov/ocohome.htm.
- Michigan Department of Natural Resources letter from James Ekdahl, Coordinator for Native American issues, to the author, September 20, 1999.
- Minnesota Department of Natural Resources letter from Rodney W. Sando, Commissioner, to Mark and Debra Zebroski, December 2, 1997.
- National Archives and Records Administration, Office of the Federal Register.
- U.S. Senate hearing before the Indian Affairs Committee, April 7, 1998.
- U.S. Supreme Court's “Visitors Guide to Oral Argument.”

Court Documents

- Brief for the Petitioners, on writ of certiorari to the United States Court of Appeals for the Eighth Circuit: *Cass County, Minnesota, et al. v. Leech Lake Band of Chippewa Indians*. Earl E. Maus, Counsel for Petitioners. October Term, 1997, Supreme Court of the U.S.
- Brief for the Citizens Equal Rights Alliance (CERA) as amicus curiae in support of Petitioners, on petition for writ of certiorari to the United States Court of Appeals for the Eighth Circuit: *County of Aitkin, et al. v. Mille Lacs Band of Chippewa Indians, et al*; *John W. Thompson, et al. v. United States of America, et al.* Douglas Y. Freeman, Counsel of Record. Lana E. Marcussen and Brian A. Thomas, Counsel for Amicus Curiae. October Term, 1997, Supreme Court of the U.S.
- Brief for Petitioners, on writ of certiorari to the United States Court of Appeals for the Eighth Circuit: *John W. Thompson, et al. v. United States of America, et al.* Gary E. Persian, Esq., Counsel of Record. Randy V. Thompson, Esq. Stephen G. Froehle, Esq. October Term, 1997, Supreme Court of the U.S.
- Supreme Court hearing, December 2, 1998.

Other Sources

- Letter from Bud Grant to the Editor of the Minneapolis *Star Tribune* regarding an editorial dated February 8, 1997.
- PERM (Proper Economic Resource Management) flier. Undated. "Wall of Fame Raffle." Minnesota Treaty case.
- Midwest Treaty Network Internet site. www.alphacdc.com/treaty/content.html, as of November 25, 1998.
- The Hunting and Angling Club, 1992 flier.

Sources

- "Summary Sheet of Policy," Lutheran Coalition for Public Policy in Minnesota, January 6, 1993.
- "Bud Grant Report," by Bud Grant, March 27, 1996.
- Letter from Frank Courteau, Lake Mille Lacs Association, Inc., to Onamia Mayor Larry Milton, dated May 18, 1998.
- "CERA Fact Sheet," Spring 1998 and *CERA News*, March, 1999. Citizens Equal Rights Alliance, Inc. www.citizensalliance.org
- Interview with Randy V. Thompson, Esq., June 23, 1999.
- Article (draft) by Julie Shortridge, free lance writer for various Minnesota newspapers. March, 1998.
- Rice University, The Center for Conservation Biology's Internet site, as of November 10, 1998.
- AAG International Research, Internet site, as of December 31, 1998.
- Greenwood Publishing Group, Inc., Internet site, as of December 23, 1998.
- Menominee Nation Internet site, as of December 10, 1998. http://www.menominee.com/nomining/home.html
- *60 Minutes* segment aired October 25, 1998.
- "Morning Edition" segment, National Public Radio, aired December 10, 1998.
- The Hartford Web Publishing Internet site, as of January 18, 1999. www.hartford-hwp.com.
- Columbus letter, March 14, 1493. The Newberry Library, Chicago.
- National Constitution Center. www.constitutioncenter.org
- Transactions & Collections of The American Antiquarian Society, 1836. Cambridge.
- News release by the Hawaiian Kingdom, August 6, 1998. www.hawaii-nation.org.
- California AIM Internet site, as of October 31, 1998. http://home.earthlink.net/~rosebud9/
- White Aryan Resistance (WAR) Internet site.

- Roland Morris, Sr., Internet site, as of January 5, 1999. http://www.ronan.net/~morris/
- *The Nationalist Observer* Internet site.
- Dr. Alan Cann of the University of Leicester, England. www.le.ac.uk/microbiology/staff/nna.html.
- Aryan Nation Internet site.
- Phone conversation with H. Shapiro, Assistant to the Solicitor General at the U.S. Department of Justice. September 1, 1999.

Sources for Maps and Graphs

- Bureau of the Census.
- Bureau of Indian Affairs.
- Bureau of Land Management.
- Central Intelligence Agency.
- *Historical Atlas of the United States*. Washington: National Geographic Society, 1993.
- Smithsonian Institution.
- U.S. Department of Commerce, Economics and Statistics Administration.
- U.S. Geological Survey.

Acknowledgments

I would like to thank all those who assisted with research, comments, information, ideas, and other forms of support and material toward completion of this book. In particular, I would like to express my gratitude to the following individuals: John Fulton Lewis, Howard and Carol Hanson, Thomas R. Jones, Alice Hershiser, Amy T. Jones, Darrel Smith, Lana Marcussen, Scott K. Morrison, Roland and Lisa Morris, Sr., Randy Thompson, Joe Fellegy, Vincent Hill, Ed Des Lauriers, and Brenda Behr.